GCSE
WJEC French

REVISION GUIDE
FOR THE NEW GCSE (2018 ONWARDS)

Bethan McHugh and
Chris Whittaker

Crown House Publishing
www.crownhouse.co.uk

First published by

Crown House Publishing Ltd

Crown Buildings, Bancyfelin, Carmarthen, Wales, SA33 5ND, UK

www.crownhouse.co.uk

and

Crown House Publishing Company LLC

PO Box 2223

Williston, VT 05495, USA

www.crownhousepublishing.com

Cover images © Alfonso de Tomás, © dikobrazik, © robodread, © lightgirl – fotolia.com

Icons, pages 4–5, 9, 11, 13, 15, 17, 106–124, © schinsilord – Fotolia.

Page 7, © LuckyImages – Fotolia. Pages 18–19, © JB Fontana – Fotolia. Page 21, © Milkos – Fotolia. Page 23, © micromonkey – Fotolia. Page 25, © julien tromeur – Fotolia. Page 26, © Photograohee.eu – Fotolia. Page 27 (t), © lassedesignen – Fotolia. Page 27 (b), © talitha – Fotolia. Pages 28–29, © Brian Jackson – Fotolia. Page 31, © BillionPhotos.com – Fotolia. Page 33 (t), © freshidea – Fotolia. Page 33 (b), © Lsantilli – Fotolia. Page 34, © WaveBreakMediaMicro – Fotolia. Page 37, © Focus Pocus LTD – Fotolia. Pages 38–39, © Iuliia Metkalova – Fotolia. Page 41, © david_franklin – Fotolia. Page 43 (t), © Robert Kneschke – Fotolia. Page 43 (b), © yatcenko – Fotolia. Page 44, © Mik Man – Fotolia. Page 47, © JackF – Fotolia. Pages 48–49, © andyastbury – Fotolia. Page 53, © Grigory Bruev – Fotolia. Page 55, © nevskyphoto – Fotolia. Page 56, © lucadp – Fotolia. Page 57, © connel_design – Fotolia. Pages 58–59, © Black Spring – Fotolia. Page 61, © Zerophoto – Fotolia. Page 63, © Delphotostock – Fotolia. Page 65 (t), © russieseo – Fotolia. Page 65 (b), © Boggy – Fotolia. Page 67, © zhu difeng – Fotolia. Pages 68–69, © peshkov – Fotolia. Page 73, © icsnaps – Fotolia. Page 75, © sanchos303 – Fotolia. Page 76, © niroworld – Fotolia. Page 77, © monkeybusiness – Fotolia. Pages 78–79, © sebra – Fotolia. Page 81, © BillionPhotos – Fotolia. Page 83, © Vladimir Melnikov – Fotolia. Page 87 (t), © Tom Wang – Fotolia. Page 87 (b), © Christian Schwier – Fotolia. Pages 88–89, © mikola249 – Fotolia. Page 91 (t), © Tamara Kulikova – Fotolia. Page 91 (b), © zhu difeng – Fotolia. Page 93, © pathdoc – Fotolia. Page 95, © djile – Fotolia. Page 97 (t), © goodluz – Fotolia. Page 97 (b), © Mila Supynnska – Fotolia. Page 99 © connel_design – Fotolia. Page 101 (t), © vege – Fotolia. Page 101 (b), © Syda Productions – Fotolia. Page 103, © faithie – Fotolia. Page 104, © Olivier Le Moal – Fotolia. Page 105, © javiindy – Fotolia.

British Library of Cataloguing-in-Publication Data

A catalogue entry for this book is available from the British Library.

Print ISBN 978-178583271-0

Printed and bound in the UK by Pureprint Group, Uckfield, East Sussex

CONTENTS

INTRODUCING WJEC GCSE FRENCH

Your French GCSE is split into three main themes:

• IDENTITY AND CULTURE
• WALES AND THE WORLD – AREAS OF INTEREST
• CURRENT AND FUTURE STUDY AND EMPLOYMENT

Your four French exams (SPEAKING, LISTENING, READING and WRITING) will cover these three themes equally. Each exam is worth 25% of your final grade. You are not allowed to use a dictionary in any exam.

Now for the confusing bit! Each of these three themes has different sub-themes which are divided into sections. These sections are all of equal importance – so don't spend all of your time concentrating on your favourites! Make sure you revise all the topics equally.

IDENTITY AND CULTURE	WALES AND THE WORLD – AREAS OF INTEREST	CURRENT AND FUTURE STUDY AND EMPLOYMENT
YOUTH CULTURE • Self and relationships • Technology and social media	**HOME AND LOCALITY** • Local areas of interest • Travel and transport	**CURRENT STUDY** • School/college life • School/college studies
LIFESTYLE • Health and fitness • Entertainment and leisure	**THE WIDER WORLD** • Local and regional features and characteristics of France and French-speaking countries • Holidays and tourism	**ENTERPRISE, EMPLOYABILITY AND FUTURE PLANS** • Employment • Skills and personal qualities • Post-16 study • Career plans
CUSTOMS AND TRADITIONS • Food and drink • Festivals and celebrations	**GLOBAL SUSTAINABILITY** • Environment • Social issues	

This revision guide covers all of the themes and sub-themes, as well as giving tips and advice on how to prepare for each exam with plenty of exam-style questions and grammar practice to help you. Bonne chance!

Note: English will be referred to throughout this revision guide as the native language in which to provide answers and to translate into/from French. If, however, you are studying WJEC GCSE French through the medium of Welsh, then please substitute 'Welsh' for 'English' accordingly.

SPEAKING EXAM

The first exam you will do is the speaking one. This is usually quite a bit earlier than the other three exams. The whole exam will last about 20 minutes, including your preparation time. This is what will happen:

1. You will go to a preparation room with an invigilator and you will be given a booklet. This booklet contains your role play, photo card and choices for the conversation. You will have 12 minutes to prepare for the exam and make notes. You can't write full sentences or a script but you should have time to think about what you are going to say and note some useful keywords and phrases.
2. Once your preparation time is up, you will go into the exam room with your teacher. You will take your notes with you. Once the teacher has recorded your name, candidate number, etc. the exam will begin. You will complete the role play, then the photo card and finally the conversation. The recording will not be stopped between each section.

ROLE PLAY

Your role play will look something like this:

Setting: Your French friend has come to visit and you are talking about health. Your teacher will play the part of your French friend.

Your teacher will speak first.

- Say what sport you do.
- Give an opinion on fast food.
- Answer the question.
- Ask your friend what he/she does to stay healthy.
- Say what you ate yesterday.

There will be a sentence at the start in English which is the 'setting' and explains the theme of the role play. Don't worry too much about the details. The most important thing is the theme – health, in this example – and the part which tells you who will speak first (usually, but not always, your teacher). There are **five** bullet points in every role play. Make sure you repond with a complete sentence for each one.

When you see **Answer the question** you will have to respond to a question you have not prepared for. In your preparation time, try to think of the sort of thing which you may be asked.

You will also have to **ask** a question. This could be quite a simple question – e.g. Fumes-tu ?

At Foundation level one of the prompts will be in a different tense (usually the past). Watch out for clues like yesterday, last year and last weekend. At Higher level there will be two prompts in a different tense. Look out for clues prompting you to use the future or conditional – e.g. tomorrow, next week, in the future.

Unlike with other parts of the speaking exam, you won't get any extra marks for adding in further details, opinions, etc. In the role play you only have to give the information asked for in the bullet points and nothing more.

You may have to give an opinion or point of view. It doesn't matter whether you really think this or not as long as you say something.

Try to answer in a complete sentence using an appropriate verb – e.g. Le fast food est super not just super.

PHOTO CARD

You will have your photo and **two** questions in advance, so there is no excuse for not having full, extended answers ready. Your teacher doesn't want you to read a script, but you should have a good idea of what to say. Your card will look something like this:

- Décris cette photo. (Foundation)/Qu'est-ce qui se passe sur cette photo ? (Higher)
- Préfères-tu fêter ton anniversaire en famille ou avec des amis ? Pourquoi ?

The first question on the photo card will always ask you to describe the photo. There is no fixed amount you have to say but you should be aiming for at least **three** or **four** details for maximum marks – e.g. Who is in the photo? What are they doing? Where are they? Why are they there? What else is in the photo? What do you think about the photo?

The second question will usually ask for an opinion. Try to elaborate as much as you can. Make sure you justify and explain your opinions and give as much information as possible.

UNSEEN QUESTIONS

Your teacher will then ask you **two** unseen questions. In the first unseen question you will usually have to comment on an opinion – e.g.:

- Je pense que les anniversaires coutent cher. Qu'en penses-tu ? I think birthdays are expensive. What do you think?

The last question will usually need to be answered in a different tense – e.g.:

- Décris ton dernier anniversaire. Describe your last birthday.

or

- Comment serait ton anniversaire idéal ? What would your ideal birthday be like?

In your preparation time try to think of some of the things you might be asked in the unseen questions. Listen carefully to what the teacher says and don't guess – if you don't understand, ask them to repeat the question. You won't lose any marks and this will buy you extra thinking time! You don't have to agree with the opinion given by the teacher.

Here are some useful phrases and questions:

À ton avis	In your opinion
Selon toi	According to you
Décris	Describe
Justifie ton opinion	Justify your opinion
Pourquoi (pas) ?	Why (not)?
Qu'en penses-tu ?/Qu'est-ce que tu en penses ?	What do you think (about it)?
Qu'est-ce que tu préfères ?	What do you prefer?
Qu'est-ce qui se passe ?	What is happening?
Quels sont les aspects négatifs/positifs ?	What are the negative/positive aspects?
Quels sont les avantages/inconvénients ?	What are the advantages/disadvantages?

CONVERSATION

The conversation lasts for 3–5 minutes (Foundation) and 5–7 minutes (Higher). This is split equally between two parts.

- Part 1 – You will be given a choice of sub-themes. You will start this part of the conversation by saying what you have chosen to talk about.
- Part 2 – This will be on a different theme and you will have a choice of sub-themes.

The conversation is your chance to show off the full extent of your knowledge of the language. What you say doesn't have to be factually correct as long as your French makes sense! You need to make sure that you are able to give some answers in the past, present and future tenses to access the highest marks. Try to give additional detail, opinions and justifications wherever possible and include some complex phrases.

If you get stuck …?

- If you don't understand a question, ask your teacher to repeat it.
- Don't worry if you can't remember a particular word, say something else instead.
- If you make a mistake, it's okay to correct yourself.

LISTENING EXAM

In the listening exam you can expect to hear different types of spoken language which may include monologues, conversations, discussions, interviews, announcements, adverts and messages.

- Before the exam starts, you will have 5 minutes reading time. Don't waste this time filling in your name and candidate number! Use the time to read the questions carefully and make sure you know what you have to do, etc. Make a note of any keywords and phrases which may be useful.
- Read the questions and make sure you are giving the required information – e.g. what, why, when, etc. Pay attention to negatives. The question 'Which hobby does she like?' requires a very different answer to 'Which hobby does she **not** like?'
- The paper will usually start with the easier questions and get harder throughout.
- You will hear each extract twice.
- There are **nine** questions but they are not all worth the same amount of marks. There are some 4, 5 and 6 mark questions so make sure you pay attention to this!
- Check carefully how many marks are available for the question. If you are asked to tick four boxes, make sure you don't tick more than four. You will lose marks if you do.
- Read the question carefully and listen to the recording for any keywords related to the question. Check the question again to make sure you are clear exactly what is being asked. Listen to the recording for a second time. Finalise your answer.
- There will be **two** questions in French on your paper. You won't know where they will be until you see your paper and they might not be next to each other. They will probably ask for an answer in the form of a tick or a letter, etc. but you might have to write something in French. If you write in English you won't get the mark, even if it's right. Always answer in the same language as the question.
- Don't leave any answers blank. Have an educated guess!

READING EXAM

In the reading exam you can expect to see a range of texts of different lengths, written in formal and informal styles and for a variety of audiences – e.g. magazine articles, information leaflets, adverts, literary texts, etc.

- Like the listening exam, the reading paper will also usually start with the easier questions and gradually get harder – but the translation from French will always be the last question.
- There will be **two** questions about literary texts. Don't worry too much about these and treat them the same as any other reading question.
- You will have **three** questions in French which, as with the listening exam, could be anywhere on the paper. You won't know where they will be until you see your paper and they might not be next to each other. They will probably ask for an answer in the form of a tick or a letter, etc. but you might have to write something in French. If you write in English you won't get the mark, even if it's right. Always answer in the same language as the question.
- Read the question carefully and scan through the text for any keywords related to the question. Check the question again to make sure you are clear exactly what is being asked.
- At Foundation level, all the questions are worth 6 marks but at Higher level there will be some harder 8 mark questions at the end of the paper.
- Don't leave any questions unanswered – try to rule out any options you are sure are wrong before making a sensible guess.
- For the translation, don't translate the text word for word – ensure your translation makes sense in the target language – and check you are correctly translating the tenses.
- Check carefully how many marks are available for the question. If you are asked to tick four boxes, make sure you don't tick more than four. You will lose marks for this.

The following is a guide to the types of rubrics and instructions that might be used in the listening and reading exams:

Choisis la réponse correcte/la bonne réponse	Choose the correct answer
Coche (✔) la bonne case	Tick (✔) the correct box
Coche (✔) les trois bonnes cases	Tick (✔) the three correct boxes
Complète les phrases/les informations en français	Complete the sentences/the information in French
Complète les phrases avec les mots de la liste	Complete the sentences with the words from the list
Écoute/Lis cette annonce	Listen to/Read this announcement/advert
Écoute/Lis cette interview/cet article/ce passage/ cette conversation/ce reportage	Listen to/Read this interview/this article/this passage/this conversation/this report
Écris deux détails	Write two details
Écris le bon prénom dans la case	Write the correct name in the box

Écris la lettre dans la bonne case	Write the letter in the correct box
Écris la bonne lettre dans chaque case	Write the correct letter in each box
Il faut remplir six cases seulement	You need to complete six boxes only
Remplis les blancs	Fill in the gaps
Qui... ?	Who ...?
Réponds aux questions en français	Answer the questions in French

WRITING EXAM

In the writing exam, try to bear the following points in mind:

- Check how many marks are available for each question so you know how to divide your time.
- See how many words you are recommended to write.
- Make a plan before you start writing.
- Always leave time to check your work.

Make sure you have:

- Been consistent with spellings.
- Used the correct gender for nouns.
- Used tenses appropriately.
- Used the correct endings for verbs.
- Included a range of sentence structures and vocabulary.
- Used a range of opinions and justifications.

Foundation: This exam is split into four questions.
- Question 1 – You will have to write six short sentences in French about the headings provided. Keep it short and simple!
- Question 2 – You will have to write approximately 50 words in total about the three bullet points provided. Try to write an equal amount for each bullet point and make sure you include opinions.
- Question 3 – You will have to write approximately 100 words in total about the three bullet points provided. You will be expected to use different tenses in this question.
- Question 4: Translation – You will have to translate five sentences into French.

Higher: This exam is split into three questions.
- Question 1 – You will have to write approximately 100 words in total about the three bullet points provided. You will be expected to use different tenses in this question.
- Question 2 – You will have to write approximately 150 words. There is a choice of two titles (**don't** write a response for both!). You will be expected to justify your ideas and points of view and use a range of tenses.
- Question 3: Translation – You will have to translate a paragraph into French.

Here are the sorts of rubrics and instructions that might be used in the writing exam. These examples are all in the **tu** form but you might get some instructions in the **vous** form if the examiners want you to write a piece of more formal French – e.g. a job application letter.

Choisis...	Choose …
Complète la fiche en français	Complete the form in French
Tu dois écrire une phrase complète	You must write a complete sentence
Donne des informations et des opinions au sujet de...	Give information and opinions about …
Écris environ 50 mots en français	Write approximately 50 words in French
Écris environ 150 mots en français	Write approximately 150 words in French
Tu dois expliquer...	You must explain …
Tu dois mentionner...	You must mention …
Présente et justifie tes idées et points de vue	Present and justify your ideas and points of view
... sur un des thèmes ci-dessous	… on one of the themes below
Tu reçois un e-mail/une lettre	You receive an e-mail/a letter
Réponds en français	Answer in French
Tu dois inclure...	You must include …
Tu peux inclure plus d'informations	You can include more information

THE BASICS

NUMBERS

CARDINAL NUMBERS

Start by learning numbers 0–30:

0	zéro	8	huit	16	seize	24	vingt-quatre
1	un	9	neuf	17	dix-sept	25	vingt-cinq
2	deux	10	dix	18	dix-huit	26	vingt-six
3	trois	11	onze	19	dix-neuf	27	vingt-sept
4	quatre	12	douze	20	vingt	28	vingt-huit
5	cinq	13	treize	21	vingt et un	29	vingt-neuf
6	six	14	quatorze	22	vingt-deux	30	trente
7	sept	15	quinze	23	vingt-trois		

Next, make sure that you can count in tens up to 100:

10	dix
20	vingt
30	trente
40	quarante
50	cinquante
60	soixante
70	soixante-dix
80	quatre-vingts
90	quatre-vingt-dix
100	cent

Make sure that you can fill in the gaps between 31–100. The same pattern continues all the way to 69:

31	trente et un	35	trente-cinq	39	trente-neuf
32	trente-deux	36	trente-six	40	quarante
33	trente-trois	37	trente-sept		
34	trente-quatre	38	trente-huit		

Then the pattern is as follows:

70	soixante-dix
71	soixante et onze

This pattern continues to 79. Then it continues as follows:

80	quatre-vingts
81	quatre-vingt-un
82	quatre-vingt-deux

This pattern continues to 89. Then it is:

90 quatre-vingt-dix
91 quatre-vingt-onze

This pattern continues to 99. From 100 and above it is:

100	cent
101	cent un
200	deux cents
211	deux cent onze
1000	mille
2000	deux mille
1,000,000	un million

Other useful numbers and quantities are:

une dizaine	about ten
une douzaine	about twelve

ORDINAL NUMBERS (FIRST, SECOND, THIRD, ETC.)

premier/première	first
deuxième	second
troisième	third
quatrième	fourth
cinquième	fifth
sixième	sixth
septième	seventh
huitième	eighth
neuvième	ninth
dixième	tenth

Ordinal numbers usually go before the noun and work like adjectives. In other words, they need to agree with the nouns they are describing – e.g. mes **premiers** jours (my **first** days).

DATES

DAYS OF THE WEEK

Days of the week don't need a capital letter in French.

lundi	Monday
mardi	Tuesday
mercredi	Wednesday
jeudi	Thursday
vendredi	Friday
samedi	Saturday
dimanche	Sunday

MONTHS

Like the days of the week, the months don't need to start with a capital letter.

janvier	January
février	February
mars	March
avril	April
mai	May
juin	June
juillet	July
aout	August
septembre	September
octobre	October
novembre	November
décembre	December

To express 'in a certain month' use the preposition **en** – e.g. Je vais en Italie **en** mars. (I'm going to Italy **in** March.)

SEASONS

le printemps	spring
l'été	summer
l'automne	autumn
l'hiver	winter
au printemps	in spring
en été	in summer
en automne	in autumn
en hiver	in winter

DATES

- Use normal numbers for dates – e.g. le six juin (the sixth of June), le trente aout (the thirtieth of August).
- Use le premier for the first of the month – e.g. le premier janvier (the first of January).

TIME

The verb **être** is used to express the time of day:

Il **est** une heure	It's one o'clock
Il **est** deux heures	It's two o'clock
Il **est** une heure cinq	It's five minutes past one
Il **est** trois heures douze	It's twelve minutes past three
Il **est** onze heures vingt	It's twenty past eleven

Minutes can be taken away from the hour (e.g. ten to, five to) using the word moins (less):

Il est une heure **moins** dix	It's ten minutes to one
Il est trois heures **moins** vingt-cinq	It's twenty-five minutes to three

You use et demi(e) (half past) et quart (quarter past) and moins le quart (quarter to):

Il est une heure **et demie**	It's half past one
Il est dix heures **et quart**	It's quarter past ten
Il est trois heures **moins le quart**	It's quarter to three

Note:

12.00	Il est midi
12.30	Il est midi et **demi**
00.00	Il est minuit
00.30	Il est minuit et **demi**
14.00	Il est quatorze heures

ASKING QUESTIONS

There are three basic ways to ask questions in French.

1. Raise your voice at the end of the statement so it becomes a question – e.g. Tu vas au restaurant ce soir ?
2. Put Est-ce que in front of the sentence – e.g. Est-ce que tu vas au restaurant ce soir ?
3. Change the subject and verb order – e.g. Vas-tu au restaurant ce soir ?

Some of the most frequently used question words are listed below:

Comment ?	How?
Que ?	What?
Qui ?	Who?
Où ?	Where?
Quel/quelle/quels/quelles ?	Which? What?
Quand ?	When?
Pourquoi ?	Why?
D'où ?	From where?
Combien ?	How much? How many?

IDENTITY
AND CULTURE

YOUTH CULTURE

The sub-theme of **Youth Culture** is divided into two areas. Here are some suggestions of topics to revise:

SELF AND RELATIONSHIPS

- family relationships
- friendships
- physical appearance and self-image
- fashion and trends
- celebrity culture
- problems and pressures of young people
- marriage

TECHNOLOGY AND SOCIAL MEDIA

- different types of technology – e.g. tablets, mobiles, smart watches
- advantages and disadvantages of technology
- advantages and disadvantages of social media – e.g. cyberbullying
- impact of social media
- computer games
- future of technology
- how you use technology

TRANSLATION TIPS

ENGLISH TO FRENCH

- Don't translate sentences word for word!
- Check you are correctly translating the tense required.

FRENCH TO ENGLISH

- Don't translate the text word for word – you don't need to have the same number of words in your translation as the original text has.
- Don't miss out little but important words – e.g. very, often, never.
- Make sure you translate the correct meaning of the tense – e.g. I play, I played, I will play, I would play. Sometimes keywords and phrases – like yesterday, in the future, later, usually – will help you to identify the tense.

SELF AND RELATIONSHIPS

Décris ta famille.
Describe your family.

J'ai une sœur qui s'appelle Sophie. Je m'entends bien avec elle parce qu'on aime la même musique. Elle est toujours amusante. J'ai aussi un frère qui est plus vieux que moi. Je pense que mes parents sont trop stricts et c'est vraiment énervant.
I have a sister called Sophie. I get on well with her because we like the same music. She is always funny. I also have a brother who is older than me. I think that my parents are too strict and that's really annoying.

Qu'est-ce que tu as fait avec tes amis le weekend dernier ?
What did you do with your friends last weekend?

Vendredi dernier, je suis allé(e) au cinéma avec mes copains de classe. Après avoir vu le film, nous sommes allés au restaurant. Nous avons mangé une pizza.
Last Friday I went to the cinema with my friends from school. After watching the film we went to a restaurant. We ate pizza.

La mode, c'est important pour toi ?
Is fashion important to you?

Oui, bien sûr. Je m'inspire des mannequins et des célébrités et j'adore acheter des vêtements. Plus tard, je voudrais travailler dans l'industrie de la mode.
Yes, of course. I'm inspired by models and celebrities and I love buying clothes. Later, I'd like to work in the fashion industry.

Est-ce qu'il y a une célébrité que tu admires ? Pourquoi ?
Is there a celebrity who you admire? Why?

J'admire Ed Sheeran parce qu'il chante bien. L'année dernière j'ai assisté à son concert. C'était fantastique.
I admire Ed Sheeran because he sings well. Last year I went to his concert. It was great.

Comment serait ton petit ami/ta petite amie idéal(e) ?
What would your ideal boyfriend/girlfriend be like?

Il/elle aurait un bon travail et il/elle serait riche et généreux/généreuse. À mon avis, avoir le sens de l'humour est important aussi.
He/she would have a good job and be rich and generous. In my opinion, it's important to have a sense of humour.

Try to use a variety of vocabulary and structures. There's no need (and you won't have enough time) to describe the colour of every member of your family's hair, eyes, etc. The vocabulary you will be using could become really repetitive.

It's easy for this topic to become too descriptive and rely mainly on present tense. Try to include some opinions – what do you think of different family members? How do you get on? Why?

Say what you did/are going to do with your family to show off your use of different tenses.

GRAMMAR

There are three important points to remember about adjectives in French:

1. Check the ending of the adjective. Is it singular (e.g. **le garçon intelligent**) or plural (e.g. **les garçons intelligents**)?
2. Check the adjective is in the right place. Most adjectives go after the noun in French (be careful – there are some exceptions!).
3. Check the agreement of the adjective. Is the noun masculine (e.g. **le garçon intelligent**) or feminine (e.g. **la fille intelligente**)?

EXAM TASK

Translate the sentences into English:

1. Ma tante est amusante, sympa et sportive.
2. Quand j'étais plus jeune, j'avais beaucoup d'amis.
3. Mon meilleur ami s'entend bien avec ses parents.
4. Quelles sont les qualités d'un bon ami ?

Have you translated all the information? Does the sentence you have written make sense in English?

SELF AND RELATIONSHIPS

Je m'intéresse à la mode.	I am interested in fashion.
Je préfère porter des vêtements de marques.	I prefer wearing designer clothes.
La vie des célébrités me fascine.	I am fascinated by celebrities' lives.
J'adore suivre les styles dans les magazines.	I love following the styles in magazines.
Je voudrais me marier à l'avenir.	I would like to get married in the future.
Selon moi, avoir une famille est très important.	In my opinion, having a family is very important.
En ce qui me concerne, la mode coute trop cher.	As far as I am concerned, fashion is too expensive.
Ma petite amie/Mon petit ami idéal serait/ferait/aurait...	My ideal girlfriend/boyfriend would be/would do/would have …
Je peux lui parler de tout.	I can talk to him/her about everything.
Il y a quelquefois des disputes.	There are sometimes arguments.
Mes parent s'inquiètent trop.	My parents worry too much.
Je peux toujours compter sur lui/elle.	I can always count on him/her.
On se dispute rarement.	We rarely argue.
Nous bavardons tout le temps.	We chat all the time.
Je ressemble à ma sœur.	l look like my sister.
Mes amis disent que j'ai le sens de l'humour.	My friends say I've got a sense of humour.
Les jeunes d'aujourd'hui ont beaucoup de problèmes.	Young people today have lots of problems.
Je pense que les célébrités influencent les jeunes.	I think that celebrities influence young people.
J'ai l'intention de vivre avec mes amis.	I intend to live with my friends.
Je m'entends bien avec ma sœur.	I get on well with my sister.
Je me dispute souvent avec mes parents.	I often argue with my parents.
Il/Elle me critique tout le temps.	He/She criticises me all the time.

Use and adapt expressions like these
in your speaking and writing exams to
access higher marks.

EXAM TASK

Décris cette photo. (Foundation)/Qu'est-ce qui se passe sur cette photo ? (Higher)

Sur cette photo il y a un groupe d'élèves. Ils sont au collège et ils ne portent pas d'uniforme. Je pense qu'ils bavardent au sujet de la fille qui est seule. Je crois qu'elle est victime de harcèlement scolaire. En plus, elle est triste parce qu'elle n'a pas d'amis.

In this photo there is a group of students. They are at school and they are not wearing a uniform. I think they are gossiping about the girl who is on her own. I think she is the victim of school bullying. What's more, she is sad because she doesn't have any friends.

Now can you answer these questions yourself?

- Comment sont tes amis ? What are your friends like?
- Les amis sont plus importants que la famille. Qu'en penses-tu ? Friends are more important than family. What do you think?
- Qu'est-ce que tu vas faire avec ta famille le weekend prochain ? What are you going to do with your family next weekend?

TECHNOLOGY AND SOCIAL MEDIA

Quel est ton site web préféré et pourquoi ?
What's your favourite website and why?

Je préfère Google parce que je l'utilise pour faire des recherches pour mes devoirs et mes projets scolaires.
I prefer Google because I use it to do research for my homework and my school projects.

Pour quelles raisons utilises-tu les réseaux sociaux ?
What do you use social media for?

J'adore utiliser les réseaux sociaux pour partager mes idées, rester en contact avec mes copains et me tenir au courant de tout ce qui se passe au collège.
I love using social media to share my ideas, stay in contact with my friends and keep up to date with everything that happens at school.

Quels sont les aspects négatifs de la technologie ?
What are the negative aspects of technology?

La technologie peut être dangereuse, parce qu'on peut rencontrer des personnes en ligne qui peuvent mentir au sujet de leur âge ou leur nom. Nous devrions faire attention à qui nous parlons.
Technology can be dangerous because you can meet people online who can lie about their age or their name. We should be careful who we are speaking to.

Quelle technologie as-tu utilisée hier ?
What technology did you use yesterday?

J'ai envoyé des textos à mes amis et j'ai lu un blog. Après avoir fait mes devoirs sur l'ordinateur, j'ai téléchargé un film.
I sent some texts to my friends and I read a blog. After doing my homework on the computer, I downloaded a film.

Pourrais-tu vivre sans portable ?
Could you live without a mobile phone?

Pour la plupart des jeunes, un portable est essentiel. Personnellement, je ne pourrais pas vivre sans mon portable parce que je l'utilise pour tout. Je suis vraiment accro !
For most young people, a mobile phone is essential. Personally, I couldn't live without my mobile because I use it for everything. I am really addicted!

Hopefully you should have a lot to say about this topic!

You may be so in love with technology that you can't think of any disadvantages or problems, but it's important that you can offer a range of opinions. Learn a variety of ways of giving opinions – e.g. **c'est** (it is), **je pense que** (I think that), **je trouve que** (I find that), **à mon avis** (in my opinion), **en ce qui me concerne** (as far as I'm concerned), **selon moi** (according to me) – and try to use a range of adjectives. Examiners can get fed up of everything being **intéressant** (interesting) or **ennuyeux** (boring).

EXAM TASK

Answer the questions in English.

Un portable permet aux jeunes de se connecter avec leurs amis et favorise l'autonomie[1]. Les jeunes font des échanges avec leurs amis par SMS, MMS et sur les réseaux sociaux. Les portables servent aussi pour la conversation avec leurs meilleurs amis. Il est essentiel pour les jeunes de construire[2] des liens sociaux. Les adolescents envoient en moyenne[3] quatre-vingts SMS par jour. Soixante-huit pourcent des enfants envoient des textos plusieurs fois par jour.

1 independence
2 to build, construct
3 on average

1. Write **two** advantages of having a mobile phone.
2. Write **three** ways young people use their mobile phones.
3. How many texts does a young person send each day?
   (a) 24
   (b) 80
   (c) 68

Watch out for distractors (annoying words the examiners put in to try to trick you)! There is more than one number mentioned in this text.

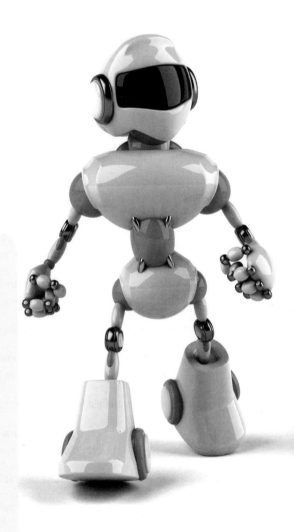

TECHNOLOGY AND SOCIAL MEDIA

Mes parents disent que je passe trop de temps sur mon portable.	My parents say I spend too much time on my mobile phone.
Je pense qu'Internet est très utile.	I think the internet is very useful.
Mes parents font des achats en ligne.	My parents shop online.
J'utilise mon portable pour télécharger et pour écouter de la musique.	I use my mobile phone to download and listen to music.
Le weekend dernier j'ai posté des photos sur les réseaux sociaux.	Last weekend I posted some photos on social media.
J'aime rencontrer des gens en ligne.	I like meeting people online.
La technologie joue un rôle important dans la vie des jeunes.	Technology plays an important role in the life of young people.
Je pense que la technologie simplifie la vie quotidienne.	I think that technology simplifies everyday life.
Ma mère croit que les réseaux sociaux sont une perte de temps.	My mum thinks social media is a waste of time.
Il est facile de se faire passer pour quelqu'un d'autre.	It's easy to pass yourself off as someone else.
La cyberintimidation est un problème très inquiétant.	Cyberbullying is a very worrying problem.
Un risque potentiel est le harcèlement sur Internet.	Harassment is a potential risk on the internet.
Je crois qu'une vie sans la technologie serait très ennuyeuse.	I think that a life without technology would be very boring.
Les portables sont très faciles à voler.	Mobile phones are very easy to steal.
Il ne faut pas révéler les détails de sa vie intime.	You shouldn't reveal details about your private life.

GRANDE

Negatives

Negative sentences are easy to form in French. Try to include some in your work – e.g. Je **ne** joue **pas** sur ma tablette.

Here are some of the common negatives you will need to understand:

ne... pas – not
ne... jamais – never
ne... plus – no longer
ne... que – only
ne... rien – nothing

Write a full sentence in French for each of the headings:

- your mobile phone
- computer games
- social media
- technology – your opinion
- music
- the internet – a disadvantage

There's no need to write a really complicated sentence. A simple sentence can score full marks even if it has some minor errors. There isn't just one correct answer – e.g. for the first bullet point you could say:

Mon portable est petit. My mobile phone is small.

Or you could even use a negative sentence:

Je n'ai pas de portable. I haven't got a mobile phone.

EXAM TASK

IDENTITY AND CULTURE

LIFESTYLE

The sub-theme of **Lifestyle** is divided into two areas. Here are some suggestions of topics to revise:

HEALTH AND FITNESS

- healthy eating
- health issues – e.g. stress, illnesses
- unhealthy lifestyle – e.g. drugs, alcohol, smoking
- sports and exercise
- benefits of a healthy lifestyle

ENTERTAINMENT AND LEISURE

- music
- cinema
- television
- shopping
- eating out
- social activities and hobbies
- work–life balance

REMEMBER:

It's really important to keep revising questions – remember that you will have to answer unpredictable questions in your speaking exam and you will also have to ask a present tense question in the role play. You also have to talk about events in the past, present and future in the photo card discussion and the conversation. It's really important that you are able to recognise questions in different tenses – e.g. **Que fais-tu d'habitude ?** (What do you usually do?), **Qu'est-ce que tu as fait hier ?** (What did you do yesterday?), **Que feras-tu demain ?** (What will you do tomorrow?) Listen out for time phrases – e.g. demain (tomorrow), hier (yesterday), etc. – that will help you answer in the correct tense.

HEALTH AND FITNESS

Que fais-tu pour rester en forme ?
What do you do to keep fit?

Je fais beaucoup de choses pour rester en forme. J'essaie de faire du sport trois ou quatre fois par semaine et je mange sainement. Après mes examens, je m'entrainerai tous les jours.
I do lots of things to keep fit. I try to do sport three or four times a week and I eat healthily. After my exams, I will train every day.

Tu préfères faire du sport ou regarder le sport ? Pourquoi ?
Do you prefer playing sport or watching sport? Why?

J'aime les deux ! Je suis une personne très sportive et je fais partie de plusieurs équipes. Cependant, j'adore regarder les matchs de foot au stade ou à la télé.
I like both! I'm a very sporty person and I am a member of several teams. However, I love watching football matches at the stadium or on TV.

Qu'est-ce qui est mauvais pour la santé ?
What is bad for your health?

Il ne faut pas fumer parce que cela peut causer des maladies graves comme le cancer des poumons. Boire de l'alcool est mauvais pour la santé aussi. Malheureusement, beaucoup de jeunes pensent que ce n'est pas un problème de boire un peu trop.
You mustn't smoke because it can cause serious illnesses like lung cancer. Drinking alcohol is bad for your health as well. Unfortunately, lots of young people don't think it's a problem to drink too much.

Que feras-tu à l'avenir pour manger plus sainement ?
What will you do in the future to eat more healthily?

Je vais essayer de manger plus de fruits et j'aimerais éviter la nourriture grasse. J'essaierai de manger un bon petit déjeuner tous les jours et je mangerai moins de chocolat.
I am going to try to eat more fruit and I would like to avoid fatty food. I will try to eat a good breakfast every day and I will eat less chocolate.

Qu'est-ce que tu as fait le weekend dernier pour garder la forme ?
What did you do last weekend to keep fit?

Samedi matin j'ai fait du jogging avec mon frère puis nous sommes allés au centre sportif pour faire de la natation. C'était fatigant !
Saturday morning I went jogging with my brother, then we went to the sports centre to go swimming. It was tiring!

GRAMMAR

Relative pronouns

A **relative pronoun** is a word used to join two parts of a sentence together when referring back to something mentioned at the beginning. They are a good way of making your sentences more complex.

- qui – who, which
- que – whom, that

e.g.:

- J'aime manger la nourriture **qui** est saine. I like eating food which is healthy.
- Quels sont les produits bio **que** vous aimez ? Which are the organic products that you like?

EXAM TASK

Answer the questions in English.

En **France**, **manger**, **boire** et grignoter prennent deux heures vingt-deux minutes par personne par jour. La plupart des gens mangent toujours les trois **repas** principaux et la moitié des français mangent le **déjeuner** vers treize heures. Quinze pourcent grignotent pendant la journée. Vingt pourcent des Français mangent devant la télé et ce sont les jeunes de vingt-quatre ans qui le font le plus. Quelques-uns aiment lire ou écouter de la musique en mangeant.

1. What is the text about?
2. What do half of French people do?
3. What do 20% of French people do?
4. What else do some French people like to do?

Question 1 is a new style of question which you can expect to see in your listening and reading exams. Try to identify some keywords (we have highlighted some in bold in this article to help you – unfortunately that won't happen in the real thing!). Make sure you read the whole text before answering the question. Don't be distracted by a few keywords towards the end of the passage – e.g. **télé**, **musique**.

HEALTH AND FITNESS

Je devrais boire plus d'eau.	I should drink more water.
J'ai décidé que je ne vais jamais fumer.	I've decided that I am never going to smoke.
Je vais manger plus de fruits et de légumes.	I am going to eat more fruit and vegetables.
Je voudrais manger moins de bonbons.	I would like to eat fewer sweets.
J'aimerais être en forme.	I would like to be fit.
Si j'avais plus d'argent, j'achèterais des produits bio.	If I had more money, I would buy organic products.
Je devrais me coucher plus tôt.	I should go to bed earlier.
Quand j'étais plus jeune, je mangeais trop de fast food.	When I was younger, I ate too much fast food.
On devrait manger cinq portions de fruits et légumes par.	You should eat five portions of fruit and vegetables a day.
Je mange toujours un bon petit déjeuner.	I always eat a good breakfast.
J'essaie de prendre des repas régulièrement.	I try to eat regular meals.
Je fais du sport/de l'exercice deux ou trois fois par semaine.	I do sport/exercise two or three times a week.
J'essaie d'avoir au moins huit heures de sommeil par nuit.	I try to have at least eight hours of sleep a night.
Beaucoup de jeunes ne font pas d'exercice en dehors de l'école.	Many young people don't do any exercise outside of school.
Il faut faire de l'exercice régulièrement et avoir une alimentation équilibrée.	You should exercise regularly and have a balanced diet.
On ne devrait pas manger trop de gras.	You shouldn't eat too much fat.
Il faut sensibiliser les jeunes aux dangers.	Young people should be made aware of the dangers.
On devient accro.	You get addicted.
Il y a plusieurs risques.	There are several risks.

Remember that you might need to use reflexive verbs when writing or speaking about this topic.

Don't forget the reflexive pronoun – e.g.:

se coucher – to go to bed
je **me** couche – I go to bed
tu **te** couches – you go to bed (singular)
il/elle **se** couche – he/she goes to bed
nous **nous** couchons – we go to bed
vous **vous** couchez – you go to bed (singular polite or plural)
ils/elles **se** couchent – they go to bed

EXAM TASK

In the role play you will have to ask a question, use the present tense and at least one additional tense and respond to an unexpected question!

Here are some examples of the prompts you might see:

- Say what you usually do to stay healthy.
- Ask your friend a question about sport.
- Give your opinion on healthy eating.
- Say what sport you did yesterday.
- Ask your friend what food he/she likes to eat.
- Say what you will do next week to stay healthy.

There are lots of different questions you could ask about sport.

You could keep it general – e.g. Tu aimes le sport ? (Do you like sport?) Tu aimes le football ? (Do you like football?)

Or be more specific – e.g. Quand joues-tu au tennis ? (When do you play tennis?) Avec qui joues-tu au basketball ? (Who do you play basketball with?)

Watch out for 'trigger' words which mean your response needs to be in a different tense – e.g. yesterday, next week.

ENTERTAINMENT AND LEISURE

Qu'est-ce que tu fais pendant ton temps libre ?
What do you do in your free time?

En ce moment je n'ai pas beaucoup de temps libre à cause de mes examens, mais ma passion c'est la natation. Je vais à la piscine au moins trois fois par semaine. Comme tout le monde je regarde la télé à la maison et je joue sur mon portable.
At the moment I don't have much free time because of my exams, but swimming is what I really love. I go to the swimming pool at least three times a week. Like everyone I watch TV at home and play on my mobile phone.

Est-ce que les passe-temps sont importants pour les jeunes ?
Are hobbies important for young people?

Oui, bien sûr. De nos jours, les jeunes ont beaucoup d'examens donc les passe-temps sont très importants pour se détendre.
Yes, of course. These days, young people have lots of exams so hobbies are really important for relaxing.

Quelle activité de loisir aimerais-tu essayer à l'avenir ?
What leisure activity would you like to try in the future?

J'aimerais faire du snowboard, parce que je ne l'ai jamais essayé et mon frère m'a dit que c'est passionnant.
I'd like to snowboard because I've never tried it and my brother told me it's exciting.

Qu'est-ce que tu as fait le weekend dernier ?
What did you do last weekend?

Samedi matin, j'ai fait la grasse matinée. Après le déjeuner, je suis allé(e) chez mon/ma meilleur(e) ami(e). Le soir, nous sommes sorti(e)s ensemble. Je me suis très bien amusé(e).
Saturday morning, I had a lie in. After lunch I went to my best friend's house. In the evening we went out together. I had a really good time.

Préfères-tu aller au cinéma ou télécharger un film à la maison ? Pourquoi ?
Do you prefer going to the cinema or downloading a film at home? Why?

Aller au cinéma coûte très cher, donc je préfère télécharger un film à la maison. En plus, mon salon est plus confortable et je peux manger et boire tout ce que je veux.
Going to the cinema is very expensive so I prefer downloading a film at home. What's more, my living room is more comfortable and I can eat and drink whatever I want.

Try to develop your answers as much as possible by adding extra detail wherever you can – e.g. to **Je vais au cinéma**...

- Add who with – Je vais au cinéma **avec mes amis.**
- Add a time phrase – Je vais au cinéma avec mes amis **le samedi.**
- Add an opinion – Je vais au cinéma avec mes amis le samedi. **C'est génial.**
- Add a justification – Je vais au cinéma avec mes amis le samedi. C'est génial, **parce que le cinéma est très moderne.**
- Add a different tense – Je vais au cinéma avec mes amis le samedi. C'est génial, parce que le cinéma est très moderne. **Samedi dernier, nous avons vu un thriller.**

EXAM TASK

Answer the questions.

Émilie : Je suis fan de la FIFA et mes parents m'achètent le jeu chaque année pour mon anniversaire. Puis le reste de l'année, ils se plaignent que je passe trop de temps à jouer !

Lila : Je suis accro aux jeux. Je préfère quand je joue avec mes amis parce que je n'aime pas jouer seule. Nous avons tous un casque micro et avec cela on peut discuter en même temps.

Jérôme : Je joue pour me reposer. Je joue souvent avec mes frères en faisant des compétitions. Je joue souvent pendant la nuit, quand mes parents pensent que je dors !

Who do you think would say the following? Émilie, Lila or Jérôme?

1. I play to relax.
2. I am addicted to games.
3. I play with my friends.
4. My parents always moan at me.
5. I play it at night.

Be careful when answering Question 4 as both Émilie and Jérôme mention their parents!

ENTERTAINMENT AND LEISURE

Il est important d'avoir des passions.	It's important to have interests.
À mon avis, les loisirs rendent la vie plus agréable.	In my opinion, leisure activities make life more enjoyable.
C'est une bonne manière d'avoir un peu de relaxation.	It's a good way to have a bit of relaxation.
L'année dernière j'avais plus de temps libre.	Last year I had more free time.
Quand je n'ai pas de devoirs, j'aime sortir avec mes copains.	When I don't have homework, I like going out with my friends.
Pendant mon temps libre, je joue au foot parce que c'est ma passion.	During my free time I play football because it's my passion.
Quand j'ai du temps libre, j'adore jouer sur l'ordinateur parce que cela me détend.	When I have free time, I love playing on the computer because it relaxes me.
Quand j'étais petit(e), je jouais de la guitarre mais je n'aime plus faire ça.	When I was small, I played the guitar but I don't like doing it anymore.
Si je n'ai pas de travail scolaire, j'essaie de faire beaucoup de choses pour me relaxer.	If I don't have any school work, I try to do lots of things to relax.
Après mes examens, j'aimerais essayer beaucoup d'activités.	After my exams, I would like to try lots of activities.
Les passe-temps nous donnent l'occasion de nous faire de nouveaux amis.	Hobbies give us the opportunity to make new friends.
J'ai l'intention de faire partie d'un club.	I intend to join a club.
Mes parents pensent que le temps libre devrait être productif.	My parents think free time should be productive.

Conjunctions

GRAMMAR

Here are some of the most commonly used **conjunctions** in French. Use them to join sentences together to improve your work.

car – for (because)
comme – as
depuis (que) – since (time)
donc – so
lorsque, quand – when
parce que – because
puisque – since (reason)
pendant que – during, while
tandis que – while

e.g.:

- Il a beaucoup joué au football **puisqu**'il voulait être footballeur professionnel. He played a lot of football since he wanted to be a professional footballer.

Translate these sentences into French:

EXAM TASK

1. Last week I went shopping in town.
2. Next weekend I am going to the cinema with my family.
3. What is your favourite TV programme?
4. I can't go out tomorrow because I have too much homework.

Remember:

- Don't translate word for word.
- Don't leave any gaps.
- Watch out for different tenses.
- Be careful with negatives.

IDENTITY AND CULTURE

CUSTOMS AND TRADITIONS

The sub-theme of **Customs and Traditions** is divided into two areas. Here are some suggestions of topics to revise:

FOOD AND DRINK

- party food and drink
- regional specialities
- eating habits
- cultural traditions
- food and drink for special occasions
- eating out

FESTIVALS AND CELEBRATIONS

- annual festivals and holidays
- birthdays
- national events
- regional events
- music festivals
- celebrating family occasions

REMEMBER:

- You need to use a variety of tenses in your written and spoken French.
- Use your verb tables to help you when you are planning your work.
- Remember to use the correct verb ending – this tells the examiner who the sentence is about. You need to use the je form to talk about yourself, but you need to learn other verb forms as well so that you can talk about other people.
- Try to include more detail by adding time expressions where possible – e.g. aujourd'hui (today), tous les jours (every day), cette semaine (this week), d'habitude (usually), hier soir (yesterday evening), la semaine dernière (last week), il y a deux mois (two months ago), demain matin (tomorrow morning), l'année prochaine (next year), dans un mois (in a month's time).

FOOD AND DRINK

Est-ce que tu aimes cuisiner ? Pourquoi (pas) ?
Do you like cooking? Why (not)?

Quand j'étais petit(e), j'aimais faire des gâteaux avec ma mère. Maintenant, je ne fais que des sandwichs ! J'aime les émissions de cuisine à la télé, mais je n'ai pas assez de temps pour faire la cuisine moi-même.
When I was younger, I liked making cakes with my mother. Now I only make sandwiches! I like cookery programmes on TV but I don't have enough time to cook myself.

Décris ton dernier repas au restaurant.
Describe your last meal at a restaurant.

Je suis allé(e) dans un restaurant italien avec mes parents le weekend dernier. J'ai choisi des pâtes et comme dessert j'ai pris une glace. Le repas était délicieux, donc j'aimerais y retourner un jour.
I went to an Italian restaurant with my parents last weekend. I chose pasta and for dessert I had an ice cream. The meal was delicious so I'd like to go back there one day.

Est-ce qu'il est important de manger les plats régionaux pendant les vacances ? Pourquoi (pas) ?
Is it important to eat regional dishes on holiday? Why (not)?

À mon avis, les touristes devraient respecter la culture de la région. Je crois qu'il est essentiel d'essayer les plats typiques. En plus, les restaurants pour touristes sont souvent très chers.
In my opinion, tourists should respect the culture of the region. I think it's essential to try local foods. What's more, tourist restaurants are often very expensive.

Comment serait ton repas idéal ?
What would your ideal meal be?

Pour mon repas idéal, je mangerais dans un restaurant sur la plage aux Caraïbes. J'essaierais des spécialités locales et je boirais des cocktails tropicaux.
For my ideal meal, I would eat in a restaurant on the beach in the Caribbean. I would try local specialities and I would drink tropical cocktails.

Que penses-tu des plats préparés ?
What do you think of ready meals?

Je mange des plats préparés de temps en temps, par exemple des pizzas surgelées, parce je n'aime pas cuisiner. Je pense que les plats préparés sont rapides et pratiques, mais je préfère les repas faits à la maison.
I eat ready meals from time to time, for example frozen pizzas, because I don't like cooking. I think ready meals are quick and practical but I prefer home-cooked meals.

You may have to talk or write about the sort of food and drink you normally have at a celebration – e.g. a birthday party. Show the examiner that you're hungry for success by showing off some different tenses and use some intensifiers to improve your work.

GRAMMAR

Intensifiers

Here are some common **intensifiers**:

assez – enough
beaucoup – a lot
un peu – a little
très – very
trop – too much
tellement – so much
extrêmement – extremely

EXAM TASK

Read this extract from a literary text. Answer the questions in English.

Le dimanche chez ma grand-mère, c'était le cérémonial : chacun avait « son » gâteau ! Moi, c'était le gâteau chocolat avec les fraises. Je ne savais pas le couper, j'en mettais partout ! Je laissais la moitié du gâteau dans l'assiette ! Petit, les mercredis après-midi dans la cuisine familiale, Christophe a lu le cahier de recettes de sa maman et a commencé ses premières expériences pâtissières.

1. Who did Christophe spend Sunday with?
2. What did he have to eat?
3. How much of it did he eat?
4. Where did he used to spend Wednesdays?

There will be two extracts from literary texts in your reading exam. Treat them just like any other reading comprehension task. Don't worry if you can't understand every single word.

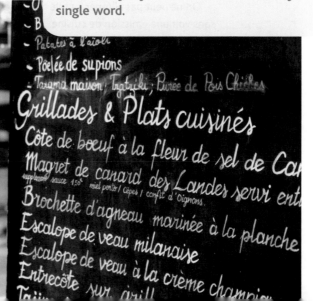

FOOD AND DRINK

Cuisiner ce n'est pas mon truc.	Cooking is not my thing.
Ma mère pense que savoir cuisiner est important.	My mum thinks that learning to cook is important.
Si j'avais le temps, j'aimerais apprendre à cuisine.	If I had the time, I would like to learn to cook.
De nos jours, on n'a pas toujours le temps et l'énergie de préparer un repas.	These days, we don't always have the time and energy to prepare a meal.
Les plats préparés sont plus caloriques et ils contiennent trop d'additifs.	Ready meals are more calorific and contain too many additives.
Mon repas préféré c'est le poulet rôti.	My favourite meal is roast chicken.
Chaque pays possède ses spécialités culinaires.	Every country has its own culinary specialities.
Les régions d'un pays devraient promouvoir leurs produits locaux.	Regions should promote their local products.
J'aime essayer de nouveaux plats.	I like trying new dishes.
Il est impossible d'aller en France sans manger de fromage.	It's impossible to go to France without eating cheese.
À mon avis, le dîner en famille est un rituel démodé.	In my opinion, eating dinner as a family is an outdated ritual.
Se retrouver ensemble autour d'une table donne l'occasion de communiquer.	Sitting around the table together gives you the chance to communicate.
Manger en famille améliore les habitudes alimentaires.	Eating as a family improves eating habits.
On ne peut pas allumer sa télé sans voir une émission de cuisine.	You can't put the TV on without seeing a cookery programme.
J'adore les émissions de téléréalité culinaires comme *Masterchef*.	I love reality cookery shows like *Masterchef*.
J'ai vraiment envie de manger au restaurant d'un chef star de la télé.	I'm really keen to eat in the restaurant of a celebrity chef.

Écris un article pour un blog. Il faut inclure :

- ton dernier repas au restaurant
- ce que tu as mangé
- tes opinions

Écris environ 100 mots en français.

Remember:
- Try to stick closely to the recommended word count in the exam.
- There is nothing to be gained by writing more than the recommended word count – in fact your work may become less accurate and you may run out of time for other questions.
- Divide your time equally between all three bullet points.
- Draft a brief plan before you start writing.
- Leave enough time to check your work otherwise you may lose marks for lack of accuracy.

Adverbs of place and time

You will need to recognise and use the following adverbs:

Place:
> dedans – inside
> dehors – outside
> ici – here
> là-bas – over there
> loin – far
> partout – everywhere

Time:
> après-demain – the day after tomorrow
> aujourd'hui – today
> avant-hier – the day before yesterday
> déjà – already
> demain – tomorrow
> hier – yesterday
> le lendemain – the following day

FESTIVALS AND CELEBRATIONS

Quelle fête préfères-tu ? Pourquoi ?
Which festival do you prefer? Why?

Ma fête préférée est le Nouvel An parce qu'on peut faire la fête toute la nuit. L'année dernière nous sommes sortis à minuit pour voir les feux d'artifice. Je me suis très bien amusé(e).
My favourite festival is New Year because you can stay up all night. Last year we went out at midnight to see the fireworks. I really enjoyed myself.

Décris une fête que tu as célébrée l'année dernière.
Describe a festival that you celebrated last year.

Pour Halloween, je me suis déguisé(e) en fantôme et j'ai fait peur à mon petit frère. C'était très amusant !
For Halloween, I dressed up as a ghost and scared my little brother. It was very funny!

Que penses-tu des fêtes traditionnelles ?
What do you think of traditional festivals?

Je suis tout à fait pour les fêtes traditionnelles, parce que ces traditions permettent de se retrouver en famille et de passer du temps ensemble. Je pense que les fêtes représentent les traditions d'une région.
I am completely for traditional festivals because these traditions allow us to meet as a family and spend time together. I think that festivals represent the traditions of a region.

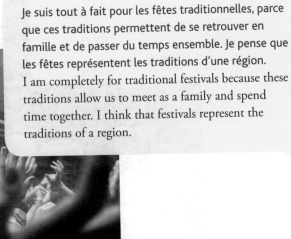

Que feras-tu pour fêter ton prochain anniversaire ?
What will you do to celebrate your next birthday?

Je fêterai mon anniversaire avec mes meilleurs copains et ma famille. Mon père me préparera un gâteau d'anniversaire et ma sœur organisera une fête à la maison. J'attends mon anniversaire avec impatience !
I will celebrate my birthday with my best friends and my family. My dad will make me a birthday cake and my sister will organise a party in the house. I can't wait for my birthday!

Est-ce qu'il y a un festival auquel tu aimerais assister ?
Is there a festival that you would like to go to?

Je n'ai jamais assisté à un festival de musique, donc après mes examens j'aimerais assister à un festival avec mes copains. Nous ferons du camping et nous verrons nos chanteurs préférés.
I've never been to a music festival, so after my exams I would like to go to a festival with my friends. We will go camping and we will see our favourite singers.

GRAMMAR

Adverbs: comparative and superlative

The main adverbs that you will need to use for comparing things are:

aussi... que – as … as
mieux... que – better … than
moins... que/de – less … than
plus... que/de – more … than

e.g.:

- Mon cadeau est **plus** grand **que** le tien. My present is bigger than yours.
- Je dépense **plus** d'argent **que** mon frère. I spend more money than my brother.

Adverbs can also be used as superlatives with le:

le mieux – the best
le plus... – the most …

e.g:

- Il chante **le mieux** ! He sings best!
- C'était **le plus** cher. It was the most expensive.

EXAM TASK

Translate the following paragraph into English:

Le festival de musique de Paris a eu lieu le premier weekend de juin. J'y suis allé avec mes amis et nous nous sommes couchés sous une tente. C'était la deuxième fois que je suis parti sans ma famille. C'était un weekend tellement incroyable ! J'aimerais y retourner l'été prochain.

The translation into English is the last question on the reading exam and is worth 6 marks – this is only 2.5% of the whole GCSE so don't spend more time on it than you would on any other question on the reading paper.

FESTIVALS AND CELEBRATIONS

D'habitude, je fête mon anniversaire avec mes amis.	Usually, I celebrate my birthday with my friends.
C'est toujours ma grand-mère qui prépare le repas traditionnel.	It's always my grandmother who makes the traditional meal.
Après le repas, nous nous offrons des cadeaux.	After the meal, we give each other presents.
J'ai eu de la chance parce que j'ai reçu beaucoup de cadeaux.	I was lucky because I received a lot of presents.
On a fait une grande fête et il y avait des feux d'artifice.	We had a big party and there were fireworks.
On a fait la fête et on a mangé un grand repas en famille.	We had a party and we had a big family dinner.
Chaque année j'envoie des cartes de vœux à tous mes amis.	Every year I send cards to all my friends.
On a beaucoup mangé et on s'est bien amusé(e)s.	We ate a lot and we had a good time.
Les fêtes traditionnelles sont des évènements culturels et historiques.	Traditional festivals are cultural and historical events.
Par contre, les fêtes sont devenues trop commerciales.	On the other hand, festivals have become too commercial.
Chez moi les traditions et les coutumes ne sont pas très importantes.	In my house traditions and customs aren't very important.
J'adore les festivals de musique parce qu'on peut voir quelques groupes et chanteurs incroyables.	I love music festivals because you can see some amazing groups and singers.
C'est une occasion fantastique de découvrir de nouvelles choses et de rencontrer beaucoup de nouvelles personnes.	It's a fantasic opportunity to discover new things and meet lots of new people.
Malheureusement, les festivals de musique sont connus pour l'utilisation de drogues et d'alcool.	Unfortunately, music festivals are known for drug and alcohol use.

EXAM TASK

Answering conversation questions on each topic in writing is good revision practice for your writing exam too.

Use and adapt the useful phrases on page 46 to help you answer the following. Remember to use a variety of tenses and to include more than one piece of information where possible. Can you justify your opinions?

- Préfères-tu fêter ton anniversaire en famille ou avec des amis ? Pourquoi ? Do you prefer celebrating your birthday with family or friends? Why?
- Les anniversaires coutent cher. Qu'en penses-tu ? Birthdays are expensive. What do you think?
- Décris ton meilleur anniversaire. Describe your best birthday.
- Comment serait ton anniversaire idéal ? What would your ideal birthday be like?
- Penses-tu que les traditions culturelles sont importantes ? Pourquoi (pas) ? Do you think that cultural traditions are important? Why (not)?
- Est-ce que tu aimes les festivals ? Pourquoi (pas) ? Do you like festivals? Why (not)?
- Quel est ton festival préféré dans ton pays ? Pourquoi ? What is your favourite festival in your country? Why?
- As-tu assisté à un festival ? Have you been to a festival?
- Comment serait ton festival de rêve ? Pourquoi ? What would your ideal party be like? Why?

GRAMMAR

En, au and aux

The words en, au and aux mean 'in' or 'to' when discussing a country.

En is used for feminine countries – e.g.:

- Le festival est **en** Irlande. The festival is in Ireland.

Au is used for masculine countries – e.g.:

- Il est **au** Canada. He is in Canada.

Aux is used for plural countries – e.g.:

- Il travaille **aux** États-Unis. He works in the USA.

WALES AND THE WORLD – AREAS OF INTEREST

HOME AND LOCALITY

The sub-theme of **Home and Locality** is divided into two areas. Here are some suggestions of topics to revise:

LOCAL AREAS OF INTEREST

- local facilities and amenities
- tourist attractions
- geographical features
- weather and climate
- advantages and disadvantages of where you live
- your local area in the past

TRAVEL AND TRANSPORT

- different types of transport
- advantages and disadvantages of types of transport
- different types of journey
- transport links
- buying tickets and booking a journey
- transport problems – e.g. delays, strikes, etc.

FORMAL LETTERS

In your writing exam, you might have to write a formal letter. You will need to set it out properly. Here are four points to remember when writing a formal letter:

1. Put your name and address top left and the name and address you are writing to top right, followed by the date underneath.
2. You start a formal letter with just Monsieur or Madame.
3. Use vous throughout the letter.
4. Use a formal ending to your letter – e.g. Je vous prie d'agréer l'expression de mes sentiments distingués.

FORMAL E-MAILS

Sending a formal e-mail in French is similar to sending a formal letter. Just begin with something simple such as Bonjour Monsieur/Madame or even just Monsieur/Madame.

End it politely, just like a formal letter, and don't forget to use vous.

LOCAL AREAS OF INTEREST

Que penses-tu de ta région ?
What do you think of your area?

Ma ville est très sale. Il y a trop de pollution à cause des voitures et des industries. Je préfèrerais habiter au bord de la mer.
My town is very dirty. There is too much pollution due to cars and industry. I would prefer to live at the seaside.

Qu'est-ce qu'il y a pour les jeunes dans ta région ?
What is there for young people in your area?

Il n'y a pas grand-chose à faire pour les jeunes. Il y a des magasins et un cinéma et c'est tout. J'aimerais avoir une piscine ou un terrain de tennis.
There isn't much to do for young people. There are some shops and a cinema and that's it. I would like to have a swimming pool or tennis court.

Que vas-tu faire dans ta région ce weekend ?
What are you going to do in your area this weekend?

Je vais retrouver mes amis au centre-ville et nous irons au cinéma. Malheureusement, il n'y a pas assez de distractions dans ma ville donc il n'y a pas beaucoup de choix pour les jeunes.
I'm going to meet my friends in the town centre and we will go to the cinema. Unfortunately, there aren't enough attractions in my town so there isn't much choice for young people.

Comment était ta région dans le passé ?
What was your area like in the past?

Il y a longtemps, ma ville était beaucoup plus petite. Mes grands-parents m'ont dit qu'il y avait beaucoup de parcs et la ville était très tranquille. Maintenant, la ville est très industrielle donc elle est plus polluée.
A long time ago, my town was much smaller. My grandparents told me that there were lots of parks and that the town was very quiet. Nowadays the town is very industrial so it is more polluted.

> Est-ce que tu aimerais changer ta région ?
> Would you like to change your area?

> Si je pouvais, je changerais de nombreuses choses dans ma ville, car il n'y a rien à faire le weekend. À mon avis, nous avons besoin d'un nouveau centre commercial.
> If I could, I would change a number of things in my town as there is nothing to do at the weekend. In my opinion, we need a new shopping centre.

It doesn't matter if you live in a huge, vibrant city or tiny village miles from anywhere. You can make up details if you need to – no one is going to come round to check whether what you have said or written is true! As well as being able to describe your local area, you need to offer opinions and discuss advantages and disadvantages.

GRAMMAR

Future plans

You can just use Je voudrais **+ infinitive** to say what you would like to do – e.g. Je voudrais habiter à l'étranger.

Or you can use the **conditional tense** to say 'would/could/should'.

To form this tense, use the stem of the future tense and the endings of the imperfect tense.

je finir**ais** – I would finish
tu finir**ais** – you would finish (singular)
il/elle finir**ait** – he/she would finish
nous finir**ions** – we would finish
vous finir**iez** – you would finish (polite singular/plural)
ils/elles finir**aient** – they would finish

EXAM TASK

Lis les informations au sujet des attractions touristiques.

A

Centre de loisirs
Café et bar
Quatre terrains de tennis
Terrain de football
Piscine couverte
Gymnase
Heures d'ouverture : 07h00–21h00 tous les jours

B

Jardins publics
Salon de thé
Parc pour enfants
Chien admis
Entrée gratuite
Piscine dehors
Heures d'ouverture : 09h00–16h00 tous les jours
(sauf le mardi)

Écris la lettre. Choisis l'attraction où on peut...

1. aller chaque jour
2. nager et faire de la musculation
3. entrer sans payer
4. nager en plein air
5. entrer six jours de la semaine

Be careful with this common type of question. Distractors are harder to spot in French! Look for different words which have the same meaning – e.g. free = without paying, every day = daily.

LOCAL AREAS OF INTEREST

USEFUL PHRASES

J'habite une des plus grandes villes d'Angleterre.	I live in one of the biggest towns in England.
Il y a beaucoup d'avantages et d'inconvénients à habiter ici. Par exemple…	There are lots of advantages and disadvantages to living here. For example …
C'est une ville très dynamique avec d'excellents transports en commun.	It's a very dynamic town with excellent public transport.
Je recommanderais une visite au printemps parce qu'il fait beau.	I would recommend a visit in spring because the weather is nice.
Ma ville est connue pour son équipe de foot très célèbre.	My town is known for its very famous football team.
Les touristes pourraient visiter la cathédrale et les musées.	Tourists could visit the cathedral and the museums.
Ma ville s'est beaucoup améliorée ces dernières années.	My town has improved a lot in the last few years.
On est en train de construire de nombreuses maisons.	Lots of houses are being built.
Si j'étais le maire de la ville, j'améliorerais la circulation.	If I were the mayor of the town, I would improve the traffic.
Si j'avais le choix, j'habiterais à la campagne.	If I had the choice, I would live in the countryside.
Pour améliorer ma région, j'investirais dans le tourisme.	To improve my area, I would invest in tourism.
Mon frère pense qu'on devrait construire un parc à thème.	My brother thinks they should build a theme park.
Je pense qu'il n'y a pas assez de choses à faire pour les jeunes.	I think that there isn't enough for young people to do.
Le samedi soir, il y a des agressions au centre-ville et il y a trop de criminalité.	On Saturday evenings there are attacks in town and there is too much crime.
Selon mes parents, il est assez difficile de trouver un logement à un prix abordable.	According to my parents, it's hard to find affordable housing.

GRAMMAR

Imperfect tense

You may need to use the **imperfect tense** to talk about what your area was like in the past or what you used to do there. The endings are:

- -ais
- -ais
- -ait
- -ions
- -iez
- -aient

Use the above endings with the stem of nous from the present tense:

Present nous form	Imperfect je form	English
nous donn**ons**	je donn**ais**	I was giving
nous finiss**ons**	je finiss**ais**	I was finishing
nous vend**ons**	je vend**ais**	I was selling

Some useful phrases for describing your area are:

c'est – it is
c'était – it was
il y a – there is/there are
il n'y a pas de – there isn't/there aren't
il y avait – there was/there were
il n'y avait pas de – there wasn't/there weren't

EXAM TASK

Translate the following paragraph into French:

I like living in my town because there are lots of things for young people to do. In the past, there wasn't a cinema but now there is a big shopping centre. In the future, I would like to live in France because I love French culture.

Check carefully that you are using the correct tenses.

TRAVEL AND TRANSPORT

Quel est ton moyen de transport préféré ? Pourquoi ?
What is your favourite type of transport? Why?

Je préfère voyager en avion, parce que c'est confortable et reposant. Malgré les accidents d'avion qui ont eu lieu récemment, l'avion est le mode de transport le plus sûr au monde.
I prefer travelling by plane as it's comfortable and relaxing. Despite the plane accidents that have happened recently, the plane is the safest method of transport in the world.

Quels sont les avantages et les inconvénients des transports en commun ?
What are the advantages and disadvantages of public transport?

Les transports en commun sont beaucoup plus efficaces. Par exemple, 50 personnes peuvent voyager à bord d'un autobus, ce qui est beaucoup mieux que 50 personnes dans des voitures séparées. Par ailleurs, c'est pratique et moins cher.
Public transport is much more efficient. For example, 50 people can travel on a bus, which is much better than 50 people in separate cars. Furthermore, it's practical and cheaper.

Quel sont les inconvénients de voyager en voiture ?
What are the disadvantages of travelling by car?

Le temps de trajet en voiture varie beaucoup en fonction de la circulation, sans oublier le problème de se garer, ce qui prend aussi du temps. Néanmoins, j'ai l'intention d'apprendre à conduire quand j'aurai dix-sept ans.
Journey time varies depending on traffic, not forgetting the problem of parking, which also takes time. Nevertheless, I intend to learn to drive when I'm seventeen.

Comment es-tu allé(e) au collège hier ?
How did you get to school yesterday?

Normalement je vais au collège à pied mais hier il pleuvait donc j'y suis allé(e) en voiture avec mes voisins.
Normally I go to school on foot but yesterday it was raining so I went by car with my neighbours.

Comment voyageras-tu en vacances l'année prochaine ?
How will you travel for your holiday next year?

L'été prochain j'irai en France avec ma famille et nous voyagerons en voiture et en bateau. J'adore le ferry, parce qu'il y a beaucoup de choses à faire pendant le voyage.
Next summer I will go to France with my family and we will travel by car and boat. I love the ferry because there are lots of things to do during the journey.

GRAMMAR

Adverbs

You might need to use **adverbs** when talking about transport in French. Adverbs are often formed in French by adding -ment to the feminine adjective – e.g.:

- rapide (quick) → rapid**ement** (quickly)
- lente (slow) → lent**ement** (slowly)

Some adverbs don't follow this pattern – e.g. souvent (often).

In French, adverbs are normally positioned after the verb (unlike in English) – e.g. Je prends **souvent** le bus (I often take the bus).

EXAM TASK

Answer the questions in English.

Nous sommes heureux de vous accueillir[1] à bord du Pont Aven. Le bureau des informations se trouve en face du restaurant. L'accès au garage est strictement interdit[2] pendant le voyage. En cas de mauvais temps, il est interdit de sortir dehors[3]. Il est interdit de fumer dans le bateau. La compagnie Brittany Ferries vous souhaite un bon voyage.

1 to welcome
2 forbidden
3 outside

1. Where can you go if you need some help?
2. Where is it exactly?
3. What is said about access to the car deck?
4. What can't you do if the weather is bad?
5. What else can't you do?

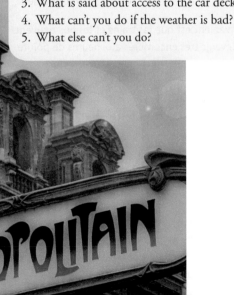

TRAVEL AND TRANSPORT

Aller au collège en voiture nous permet de partir à l'heure que nous voulons.

Going to school by car allows us to leave at the time we want.

Je n'aime pas dépendre des horaires des transports en commun.

I don't like depending on public transport timetables.

Utiliser la voiture pour aller au collège ou au travail est nuisible à l'environnement.

Using cars to travel to school or work is harmful to the environment.

Si on habite dans une grande ville, les transports en commun sont la plupart du temps la solution la plus rapide.

If you live in a big town, public transport is often the quickest solution.

Si on trouve une place assise dans le train, on peut lire tranquillement un livre.

If you find a seat on the train, you can read a book quietly.

Si on a la chance de ne pas habiter trop loin du collège, on peut simplement y aller à pied ou à vélo.

If you are lucky enough to live not too far from school, you can simply go there on foot or by bike.

À mon avis, aucun autre moyen de transport n'est aussi écologique que le vélo.

In my opinion, there is no other method of transport as environmentally friendly as a bike.

Aller à pied contribue à un environnement plus propre, et on se déplace gratuitement.

Walking contributes to a cleaner environment, and you can travel for free.

Certains modes de transport nuisent à la santé, à la qualité de vie et à l'environnement.

Certain methods of transport are harmful for health, quality of life and the environment.

Un inconvénient est que les trains et les bus peuvent devenir très encombrés aux heures de pointe.

One disadvantage is that trains and buses can get very crowded at rush hour.

This topic isn't just about buying a ticket! You need to be able to give opinions on different types of transport and make comparisons between them. Think of ways to include the past, present and future tenses in your answers.

In the exam the first question on the photo card will ask you to describe the photo (or what is happening in it):

• Décris cette photo. (Foundation)/Qu'est-ce qui se passe sur cette photo ? (Higher)

The second question will usually ask you for an opinion – e.g.:

• Est-ce qu'il y a assez de pistes cyclables dans ta région ? Pourquoi (pas) ? Does your area have enough cycle lanes? Why (not)?

Your teacher will then ask you **two** unseen questions. In the first unseen question you will usually have to comment on an opinion – e.g.:

• Les transports publics ne coutent pas cher. Qu'en penses-tu ? Public transport isn't expensive. What do you think?

The last question will usually need to be answered in a different tense – e.g.:

• Quelles moyennes de transport as-tu utilisés la semaine dernière ? Which types of transport did you use last week?

In your preparation time, try to think of some of the things you might be asked in the unseen questions.

WALES AND THE WORLD – AREAS OF INTEREST

THE WIDER WORLD

The sub-theme of **The Wider World** is divided into two areas. Here are some suggestions of topics to revise:

LOCAL AND REGIONAL FEATURES AND CHARACTERISTICS OF FRANCE AND FRENCH-SPEAKING COUNTRIES

- places of interest in French-speaking countries
- geographical features
- weather and climate
- tourist attractions and monuments
- regional characteristics

HOLIDAYS AND TOURISM

- holiday locations and resorts
- types of holiday
- holiday accommodation
- holiday activities
- advantages and disadvantages of tourism
- different types of tourism
- problems and complaints

REMEMBER:

You will be marked for linguistic knowledge and accuracy in your speaking and writing exams. It is important to spend time revising basic things like:

- genders of nouns
- verb endings
- adjectives (and agreements)
- prepositions
- tenses

You are not expected to be an expert on every tourist attraction in France, but you should be able to talk generally about the topic.

LOCAL AND REGIONAL FEATURES AND CHARACTERISTICS OF FRANCE AND FRENCH-SPEAKING COUNTRIES

Est-ce que tu es déjà allé(e) en France ?
Have you ever been to France?

Je n'ai jamais visité la France, mais j'ai envie d'aller à Paris pour monter à la Tour Eiffel. J'adore les parcs d'attractions, donc je voudrais aussi aller à Disneyland Paris.
I've never visited France but I'm keen to go to Paris to go up the Eiffel Tower. I love theme parks so I would like to go to Disneyland Paris as well.

Est-ce que tu aimes visiter les monuments historiques ? Pourquoi (pas) ?
Do you like visiting historical monuments? Why (not)?

Je suis de l'opinion qu'on doit être curieux au sujet de l'histoire d'une région, mais je trouve les musées un peu ennuyeux. Ce qui me plait, c'est acheter des souvenirs.
I'm of the opinion that you should be curious about the history of an area, but I find museums a bit boring. What I enjoy is buying souvenirs.

Quel pays francophone aimerais-tu visiter ? Pourquoi ?
Which French-speaking country would you like to visit? Why?

J'aimerais visiter l'ile Maurice, qui se trouve dans l'océan Indien, parce que les plages sont très belles là-bas. Malheureusement, les vacances à l'ile Maurice coutent très cher.
I would like to visit Mauritius, which is in the Indian Ocean, because the beaches are very beautiful there. Unfortunately, holidays to Mauritius are very expensive.

If you've never been to France or a French-speaking country you can either make up a visit so you've got something to talk about or describe where you'd like to visit! There is a lot of overlap with the vocabulary you'll need for **local areas of interest**, just in a different context.

Décris une visite d'une attraction touristique que tu as faite récemment.
Describe a recent visit you made to a tourist attraction.

Le weekend dernier, nous avons fait une excursion au château. Il y avait trop de touristes mais nous nous sommes bien amusé(e)s.
Last weekend, we went on a trip to the castle. There were too many tourists but we had a good time.

Est-ce qu'il est important d'apprendre l'histoire d'une région quand on est en vacances ? Pourquoi (pas) ?
Is it important to learn about the history of an area when you're on holiday? Why (not)?

Je pense que les touristes devraient respecter les différentes cultures. Par contre, si on n'aime pas l'histoire, on ne devrait pas être obligé de visiter les musées et les monuments.
I think that tourists should respect different cultures. On the other hand, if you don't like history you shouldn't have to visit museums and monuments.

GRAMMAR

Prepositions
In French there is often more than one way of translating a preposition.

For example, **in** could be translated into French as dans, en or à.

Here are three of the most common prepositions:

1. Before
avant (before) – e.g. **avant** le dîner
déjà (already) – e.g. Je l'ai **déjà** vu.
devant (in front of) – e.g. **devant** le château

2. In
à – e.g. **à** Lyon
dans – e.g. **dans** un magasin
en – e.g. **en** France

3. On
à – e.g. **à** gauche
en – e.g. **en** vacances
sur – e.g. **sur** les réseaux sociaux

EXAM TASK

Translate the following paragraph into English:
L'année dernière, je suis allée en vacances avec mes parents. Nous avons logé chez ma tante qui habite au bord de la mer. Nous lui avons rendu visite en juillet. Il faisait très chaud. Nous avons beaucoup aimé la plage. Le parc d'attractions était vraiment super et je voudrais y retourner l'été prochain.

Make sure you check that your English makes sense. Don't forget that the word order could be different in French.

LOCAL AND REGIONAL FEATURES AND CHARACTERISTICS OF FRANCE AND FRENCH-SPEAKING COUNTRIES

Je pense qu'aller à l'étranger est essentiel parce qu'on peut découvrir de nouvelles cultures ou pratiquer une langue étrangère.

I think going abroad is essential because you can discover new cultures or practise a foreign language.

Si on aime l'histoire, il y a des musées d'art et des monuments historiques.

If you like history, there are art museums and historical mouments.

Les touristes peuvent visiter des sites intéressants comme le château.

Tourists can visit interesting sites like the castle.

Les attractions touristiques de Paris font partie des plus visitées au monde.

The tourist attractions of Paris are some of the most visited in the world.

La ville attire en effet des millions de visiteurs chaque année.

The town attracts millions of tourists every year.

C'est une ville historiquement riche et on y trouve plusieurs monuments anciens.

It's a town rich in history and there are lots of ancient monuments there.

Les nombreux monuments historiques sont des témoins précieux du passé.

The numerous historical monuments are precious reminders of the past.

La France est une destination de rêve pour les visiteurs qui s'intéressent à l'histoire.

France is a dream destination for visitors who are interested in history.

L'histoire de France est connue dans le monde entier et beaucoup de touristes ont envie de visiter le pays.

The history of France is known throughout the world and lots of tourists want to go there.

Les parcs d'attractions comme Disneyland Paris et le Futuroscope deviennent de plus en plus populaires.

Theme parks like Disneyland Paris and Futuroscope are becoming more and more popular.

La France est célèbre pour ses vins, sa cuisine et sa culture.

France is famous for its wines, its cooking and its culture.

C'est une ville dynamique et vibrante qui offre une multitude d'opportunités.

It's a dynamic and vibrant town that offers a multitude of opportunities.

À mon avis, c'est un pays qui offre un choix de destinations avec des identités régionales.

In my opinion, it's a country that offers a choice of destinations with regional identities.

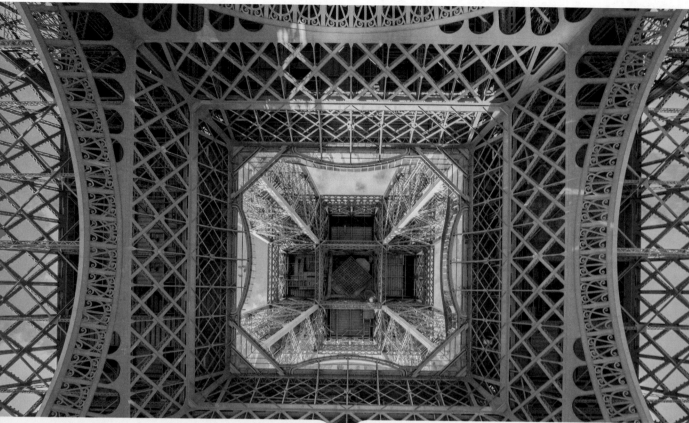

Infinitives

Verbs in French can often be followed by an infinitive – e.g.:

- Je sais nager. I can swim.
- Tu veux venir ? Do you want to come?

Many verbs need to use a preposition when they are followed by an infinitive. Here are some of the common ones:

> aider à – to help to
> apprendre à – to learn to
> commencer à – to begin to
> continuer à – to continue
> décider de – to decide to do something
> inviter à – to invite to
> ressembler à – to resemble
> réussir à – to succeed in
> s'arrêter de – to stop (doing)
> avoir l'intention de – to intend to
> avoir peur de – to be afraid of (doing)
> avoir besoin de – to need to

Here are some examples of role play prompts on this topic.

- Say what the weather is like.
- Say what you normally do on holiday.
- Ask your friend a question about a tourist attraction.
- Ask your friend what they like to do on holiday.
- Say where you went last year.
- Say what tourist attraction you will visit next year.

Remember that you what you say doesn't have to be factually accurate, as long as your French is correct. It's okay to make up answers.

You don't need to give extra information. For the first bullet point you could say something as simple as Il fait beau to score full marks.

Que fais-tu normalement pendant les vacances ?
What do you normally do during the holidays?

Nous allons en vacances pendant quinze jours chaque année. Nous partons en famille et quelquefois mes cousins viennent aussi. Nous faisons du camping ou nous logeons dans une caravane. Ma mère utilise Internet pour faire des recherches et réserver un logement pas cher.
We go on holiday for a fortnight every year. We go as a family and sometimes my cousins come too. We go camping or we stay in a caravan. My mum uses the internet to find and book cheap accommodation.

Quels sont les aspects positifs du tourisme ?
What are the positive aspects of tourism?

Le tourisme est bon pour l'économie de la région. En plus, c'est une très grande industrie qui aide à sauvegarder les traditions.
Tourism is good for the economy of the region. What's more, it's a big industry that helps to safeguard traditions.

Que préfères-tu ? Les vacances au bord de la mer ou en ville ? Pourquoi ?
What do you prefer? Holidays at the seaside or in town? Why?

Je préfère la plage parce que j'adore nager et j'aime tous les sports nautiques. Pour moi, c'est important de faire une activité. Par exemple, l'année dernière j'ai appris à faire de la planche à voile.
I prefer the beach because I love swimming and I like all water sports. It's important for me to do an activity. For example, last year I learned to windsurf.

Quelles activités as-tu faites pendant tes vacances dernières ?
What activities did you do during your last holiday?

Pendant la journée, nous sommes allé(e)s à la plage et j'ai appris à faire du surf. Un jour, nous avons fait une excursion en ville et j'ai acheté des souvenirs pour mes amis. C'était super !
During the day, we went to the beach and I learned to surf. One day, we went on a trip to town and I bought souvenirs for my friends. It was great!

Comment seraient tes vacances de rêve ?
What would your dream holiday be like?

Mes vacances idéales seraient d'être avec toute ma famille sur une île où il ferait toujours du soleil et il y aurait du sable blanc. Je rêve d'un hôtel de luxe avec une piscine énorme.
My ideal holiday would be with all my family on an island where it would be sunny every day and there would be white sand. I dream of a luxury hotel with an enormous swimming pool.

EXAM TASK

Lis les textes. Écris le bon nom.

Nathan : Je ferai du surf cette année. Ce sera ma première fois ! Je crois que je vais souvent tomber dans l'eau !

Laetitia : Pour moi c'est toujours le volleyball ! Je suis très sportive et je n'aime pas prendre de bains de soleil à la plage.

Carl : J'adore nager, je suis dans l'eau tout le temps ! Je n'ai jamais fait de surf.

Mathieu : Je me cache sous ma serviette et je dors !

Qui... ?

1. fait de la natation
2. n'aime pas se faire bronzer
3. va faire du sport nautique
4. se repose

You should feel confident about using the past, present and future tenses in your spoken and written French.

You can also add in a variety of other tenses and expressions to extend your answers. For example:

- The present tense to talk about activities you do regularly – e.g. Je vais à la plage.
- The imperfect tense for things that used to happen regularly in the past – e.g. Il pleuvait souvent.
- The perfect tense to say what you have done – e.g. Nous sommes allés à Barcelone.
- The immediate future to say what you are going to do – e.g. Ce soir je vais jouer au tennis.
- The future tense to say what you will do – e.g. J'irai en Italie.
- The conditional tense to say what you would do – e.g. J'aimerais aller à la montagne.

You don't have to use all of these tenses in all of your answers, but you do need to be able to recognise them as they will appear in your listening and reading exams. You will need to refer to past, present and future events in your speaking and writing exams.

HOLIDAYS AND TOURISM

Les vacances, c'est le meilleur moment de l'année.	Holidays are the best time of the year.
Pour moi il est essentiel d'aller à l'étranger.	For me it's essential to go abroad.
Ce que je préfère c'est me faire bronzer à la plage.	What I prefer doing is sunbathing on the beach.
D'habitude nous faisons du camping, puisque les hôtels sont trop chers.	Usually we go camping because hotels are too expensive.
Quand j'étais petit(e) je restais avec mes parents, mais maintenant je préfère passer mes vacances avec mes copains.	When I was younger I stayed with my parents but now I prefer spending my holidays with my friends.
Je préfère partir en vacances en hiver, parce que j'aime aller à la montagne pour faire du ski.	I prefer going on holiday in winter because I like going to the mountains to ski.
C'était vraiment une expérience inoubliable.	It really was an unforgettable experience.
Mes vacances étaient reposantes, car l'hôtel était tellement confortable.	My holidays were relaxing because the hotel was so comfortable.
J'aurais préféré aller ailleurs.	I would have preferred to go elsewhere.
Je dois admettre que j'ai été choqué(e), parce qu'il n'y avait pas de connexion wifi.	I must admit I was shocked, because there was no wifi.
En arrivant nous sommés allé(e)s à la piscine tout de suite.	On arriving we went to the swimming pool straight away.
Nous étions sur le point d'aller à la plage quand il a commencé à pleuvoir.	We were about to go to the beach when it started to rain.
Le tourisme peut être mauvais pour l'environnement.	Tourism can be bad for the environment.
Il y a des touristes qui sont sales et bruyants et ils jettent leurs déchets par terre.	There are some tourists who are dirty and noisy and they throw their rubbish on the floor.
Le tourisme favorise l'emploi et le développement d'une région.	Tourism offers employment and development for an area.
Les immeubles et hôtels construits pour les touristes gâchent le paysage.	The buildings and hotels built for tourists spoil the landscape.

GRAMMAR

Tenses

Complete each sentence using the specified tense of the verb in brackets.

1. L'année dernière, je _____
   (**aller** – perfect) en Espagne.
2. Il _____ (**faire** – imperfect)
   beau et le soleil _____ (**briller** –
   imperfect).
3. Nous _____ (**passer** –
   perfect) deux nuits dans un hôtel au bord de la
   mer.
4. Normalement, je _____ (**faire** –
   present) beaucoup d'activités nautiques.
5. L'été prochain, nous _____
   (**voyager** – future) en avion.

EXAM TASK

Write a full sentence in French for each of the headings:

- transport
- accommodation
- weather
- meals
- activities
- your opinion

Make sure your sentence is complete and contains an appropriate verb – e.g. for the first bullet point you should say **Je vais en avion** not just **en avion**.

WALES AND THE WORLD – AREAS OF INTEREST

GLOBAL SUSTAINABILITY

The sub-theme of **Global Sustainability** is divided into two areas. Here are some suggestions of topics to revise:

ENVIRONMENT

- environmental issues
- recycling
- climate change
- drought and flooding
- pollution
- types of energy
- environmental groups

SOCIAL ISSUES

- charity events
- raising money
- worldwide problems – e.g. poverty, famine, health, homelessness
- volunteering

ADVICE

A task on the environment or social issues might seem harder than some of the other sub-themes. You will need to learn some topic-specific vocabulary but the expectations are the same as with all the other sub-themes. You need to express opinions and refer to events using the past, present and future tenses. Try to write extended sentences using connectives. You can combine more than one tense in a sentence and you can vary the vocabulary that you use to express opinions. When revising this sub-theme, it might be helpful to think of how you could do the following:

- express which social or environmental problems you are worried about and why
- talk about a charity you support and what it does
- talk about something that happened in the past – e.g. a charity event you attended
- say what you do at the moment to support charities or help the environment
- talk about a future event – e.g. a cake sale you will organise, a fundraiser you will attend, your plans to volunteer, how you will become more eco-friendly, etc.
- say how young people can help or what people should do to help

ENVIRONMENT

Quels sont les problèmes environnementaux dans ta région ?
What are the environmental problems in your area?

Malheureusement, il y a beaucoup de problèmes dans ma région. D'abord, il n'y pas assez de poubelles, donc beaucoup de gens jettent leurs déchets par terre. Aussi je pense que, dans les rues, il y a trop de voitures qui contribuent à la pollution de l'air.
Unfortunately, there are lots of problems in my area. Firstly, there aren't enough bins, so a lot of people throw their rubbish on the street. Also, I think there are too many cars on the roads which contribute to air pollution.

À ton avis, qui est responsable des problèmes environnementaux ?
In your opinion, who is responsible for the environmental problems?

Je pense que le gouvernement doit informer la population sur les problèmes environnementaux et nous donner plus d'informations pour éduquer les jeunes. Néanmoins, nous sommes tous responsables de notre environnement.
I think that the government must inform the population about environmental problems and give us more information to educate young people. Nevertheless, we are all responsible for our environment.

Penses-tu que le recyclage est important ? Pourquoi (pas) ?
Do you think recycling is important? Why (not)?

Bien sûr, le recyclage est très important pour notre environnement et pour l'avenir de notre planète. Le recyclage nous permet, avant tout, d'économiser les ressources naturelles.
Of course, recycling is very important for our environment and for the future of our planet. Above all, recycling allows us to save natural resources.

Décris la dernière chose que tu as faite pour protéger l'environnement.
Describe the last thing you did to protect the environment.

Ce matin j'ai pris une douche au lieu d'un bain pour ne pas gaspiller l'eau. Aussi, j'ai choisi des produits locaux pour mon petit déjeuner.
This morning I had a shower instead of a bath so as not to waste water. Also I chose local products for my breakfast.

Es-tu « écolo » ? Pourquoi (pas) ?
Are you 'green'? Why (not)?

Je fais de mon mieux mais je ne suis pas parfait(e). C'est assez difficile de renoncer aux produits non-biodégradables, mais j'essaie d'utiliser plus de produits naturels et moins de produits chimiques.
I do my best but I'm not perfect. It's quite difficult to give up non-biodegradable products, but I try to use more natural products and fewer chemical products.

Qu'est-ce qu'on devrait faire pour protéger l'environnement ?
What should we do to protect the environment?

En général, nous devrions modifier la manière dont nous utilisons notre énergie. À la maison, on devrait baisser le chauffage et éteindre les lumières quand on sort d'une pièce pour économiser l'électricité.
In general, we should change the way we use energy. At home, we should turn the heating down and switch off lights when we leave a room to save electricity.

The following are useful verbs for talking about the environment. Can you translate them into English? Can you write a sentence using each one? Vary your tenses where possible.

- aider
- protéger
- réduire
- endommager
- sauver
- polluer
- recycler
- détruire
- causer
- gaspiller
- utiliser

GRAMMAR

Depuis

Remember that **depuis** can be used with the present tense and a time phrase to mean 'has/have been' – e.g.:

- Je recycle **depuis** quatre ans. I have been recycling for four years.

Depuis can also be used with the imperfect tense and a time phrase to mean 'had been …' – e.g.:

- Il travaillait pour Greenpeace **depuis** trois ans. He had been working for Greenpeace for three years.

EXAM TASK

Match 1–6 to a–f.

La plupart de nos déchets[1] ne sont pas biodégradables et ils mettent de nombreuses années à se décomposer. Voici des statistiques :

Les vêtements en nylon mettent trente à quarante ans à se décomposer[2].

Pour le papier et le journal, cela prend deux à trois mois et pour un chewing-gum c'est cinq ans !

Parmi les pires[3], il y a les sacs ou les bouteilles en plastique qui mettent cent à cinq cents ans à se décomposer !

Les pires, ce sont les bouteilles en verre qui mettent quatre mille ans à disparaître[4] et les piles qui mettent huit mille ans !

1 waste
2 to decompose
3 among the worst
4 disappear

Product	How long they take to break down
1. plastic	a. 30–40 years
2. batteries	b. 100–500 years
3. chewing gum	c. 8000 years
4. clothes	d. 5 years
5. paper	e. 2–3 months
6. glass bottles	f. 4000 years

ENVIRONMENT

J'essaie d'acheter les produits issus du commerce équitable.	I try to buy fair trade products.
Je prends un sac réutilisable et je prends les transports en commun quand je fais mes courses.	I take a reusable bag and I take public transport when I go shopping.
On devrait conserver les ressources naturelles et utiliser les énergies renouvelables.	We should conserve natural resources and use renewable energy.
Chez moi, je recycle le carton, le papier et le verre.	At home, I recycle card, paper and glass.
On ne peut pas ignorer les statistiques choquantes.	We can't ignore the shocking statistics.
Il faut faire le point sur le développement durable.	We need to focus on sustainable development.
Selon les experts, l'impact de la perte de la biodiversité sera énorme.	According to experts, the impact on biodiversity will be enormous.
Le secret ne réside pas toujours dans les grandes actions mais les petites choses qu'on fait tous les jours.	The secret isn't always in big actions but in the little things we do every day.
Ce qui me préoccupe le plus, c'est l'effet de serre.	What worries me the most is the greenhouse effect.
La pollution atmosphérique sera un problème grave pour l'environnement à l'avenir.	Atmospheric pollution will be a serious problem for the environment in the future.
La destruction de la forêt amazonienne deviendra un problème très grave.	The destruction of the Amazon rainforests will become a very serious problem.
C'est triste qu'il y ait beaucoup d'animaux en voie d'extinction.	It's sad that there are lots of endangered animals.
À l'avenir, je continuerai à réutiliser autant que possible, parce que je pense que c'est très important.	In the future I will continue to reuse as much as possible because I think it's very important.
Nous avons besoin d'un centre de recyclage et de plus d'espaces vertes dans notre ville.	We need a recycling centre and more green spaces in our town.
Les gens sont devenus de plus en plus conscients de l'importance de l'environnement.	People have become more and more conscious of the importance of the environment.
Quand j'étais petit(e), je ne faisais rien pour protéger la planète.	When I was little, I didn't do anything to protect the planet.

Write a sentence to describe an environmental problem using each of the following adjectives.

Remember to make them agree with the noun they are describing.

mondial – worldwide
dangereux – dangerous
nocif – harmful
grave – serious
inquiétant – worrying

EXAM TASK

Écris un dépliant au sujet de l'importance d'être écolo. Il faut inclure :

- Ce que tu fais pour être écolo
- L'importance de sauver la planète
- Ce que tu vas faire à la maison pour protéger l'environnement

Aim to write approximately 100 words. Try to stick within this limit. There are no extra marks for writing more than this! The second bullet point is asking for your opinions – try to justify them as much as possible. The third bullet point requires you to use the future tense.

SOCIAL ISSUES

Quel est le problème social qui t'inquiète le plus ?
What is the social problem that worries you the most?

En ce qui me concerne, le plus grand problème du monde c'est le chômage. Je crois que les pays d'Europe doivent faire plus pour améliorer la situation.
As far as I'm concerned, the biggest problem in the world is unemployment. I think that the countries of Europe must do more to improve the situation.

Qu'est-ce qu'on peut faire pour résoudre les problèmes de pauvreté ?
What can we do to solve the problems of poverty?

Malheureusement, il n'y a pas de solution facile. Tout le monde devrait faire quelque chose, par exemple, donner de l'argent aux associations caritatives.
Unfortunately, there isn't an easy solution. Everyone should do something, for example, giving money to charities.

Est-ce que le gouvernement devrait aider les sans-abris ? Pourquoi (pas) ?
Should the government help the homeless? Why (not)?

Je pense qu'il faut absolument combattre le problème des sans-abris. À mon avis, le gouvernement devrait construire plus de logements sociaux et créer plus d'emplois.
I think we must absolutely fight homelessness. In my opinion, the government should build more social housing and create more jobs.

Qu'est-ce que tu as fait récemment pour aider les autres ?
What have you done recently to help other people?

J'ai contribué à une organisation caritative et j'ai aidé à organiser une vente de gâteaux au collège.
I contributed to a charity and I helped to organise a cake sale at school.

Qu'est-ce que tu aimerais faire pour aider les autres ?
What would you like to do to help other people?

Je voudrais aider les enfants défavorisés et, après mes examens, j'ai l'intention de collecter de l'argent et de faire du bénévolat.
I would like to help underprivileged children and, after my exams, I intend to raise money and do voluntary work.

How to talk about social issues:

- Say which global issues worry you and use appropriate verbs to give your opinions – e.g. ce qui m'inquiète c'est... You could explain what kind of problems each issue causes or how it affects people, and you could also say what you think will happen in the future.
- You need to give several reasons why it's important to help other people. You could also mention what you have done recently to help other people – e.g. charity events at school, raising money, volunteering. Don't worry if you haven't done any of these things – just make it up!
- You can also mention what individuals can do – e.g. tout le monde peut..., or should do – e.g. tout le monde devrait..., and what the government should do – e.g. le gouvernement devrait... This is a good opportunity to include the subjunctive if you can – e.g. Le problème le plus grave que nous ayons rencontré chez nous, c'est les SDF (sans domicile fixe).

EXAM TASK

Answer the questions in English.
Est-ce que tu es lycéen(ne) ?
As-tu entre seize et dix-huit ans ?
Est-ce que tu veux changer des choses ?
Nous avons mille jeunes ambassadeurs en France qui aident l'UNICEF et les enfants défavorisés dans le monde. Si tu penses que tu peux nous aider, contacte-nous sur le site web, www.unicef.fr.

1. What are the **three** questions asked?
2. How many young ambassadors does UNICEF France have?
3. Who does the charity help?
4. How can you apply to be an ambassador?

Read the text once, then read the questions, then read the text again. Use cognates (words that are similar to English ones) or near cognates to help you work out the meaning of certain words.

SOCIAL ISSUES

De nos jours, le problème du chômage devient plus inquiétant.

These days, the problem of unemployment is becoming more worrying.

Il y a des milliers de gens qui n'ont pas assez à manger.

There are thousands of people who haven't got enough to eat.

Notre gouvernement devrait donner de l'aide aux pays en voie de développement.

Our government should give aid to developing countries.

C'est un problème qui touche un grand nombre de pays européens.

It's a problem which affects a large number of European countries.

Au cours des dernières années on a vu le problème s'amplifier.

Over the last few years we have seen the problem increase.

Il est nécessaire de protéger les droits de l'homme.

It's necessary to protect human rights.

Les SDF sont confrontés à de nombreux problèmes tels que la faim, le chômage et l'alcoolisme.

Homeless people are faced with numerous problems such as hunger, unemployment and alcoholism.

Il faut promouvoir l'égalité des chances et lutter contre le racisme.

We must promote equal opportunities and fight against racism.

J'aimerais aller à une manifestation pour protester contre la discrimination.

I would like to go to a demonstration to protest against discrimination.

En vérité, ce problème menace notre société.

In fact, this problem threatens our society.

Le gouvernement devrait consacrer plus d'argent à combattre ces problèmes.

The government should commit more money to fight these problems.

Il y a beaucoup de gens qui pensent qu'il faut aider les enfants défavorisés.

There are lots of people who think that we must help underprivileged children.

Beacoup de gens sont victimes de la crise économique.

Many people are victims of the economic crisis.

Il faut faire plus pour résoudre le problème du chômage.

More must be done to solve the problem of unemployment.

Top tips for the conversation:

- Listen carefully to the question. Work out whether the question asked uses the present, past or future tense so that you can use the same tense in your answer.
- Speak clearly and loudly.
- Don't worry if you hesitate. Don't use 'umm' or 'err' as we do in English but try to use some French words instead, for example alors... or ben...
- Give a reason or an opinion wherever possible – don't just answer 'yes' or 'no' – oui ou non. Learn three different ways of expressing 'I think that' or 'in my opinion' in French and try to use them in your answers.
- Say lots! The conversation is your chance to show what you can do.

EXAM TASK

Here are some possible questions for which you can prepare answers. Practise them aloud and work on your accent.

- Quels sont les problèmes sociaux qui t'inquiètent le plus ? Which social issues concern you the most?
- Quelle est ton organisation caritative préférée ? Pourquoi ? Which is your favourite charity? Why?
- Comment est-ce qu'on peut aider les personnes défavorisées ? How can you help underprivileged people?
- Qu'est-ce que tu as fait au collège pour aider les autres ? What have you done at school to help others?
- Que fais-tu pour les organisations caritatives ? What do you do for charities?
- Que feras-tu à l'avenir pour aider les organisations caritatives ? What will you do in the future to help charities?

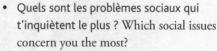

CURRENT AND FUTURE STUDY AND EMPLOYMENT

CURRENT STUDY

The sub-theme of **Current Study** is divided into two areas. Here are some suggestions of topics to revise:

SCHOOL/COLLEGE LIFE

- school day
- comparison of the school system in different countries
- school facilities
- school trips
- clubs
- rules and regulations
- advantages and disadvantages of school uniform

SCHOOL/COLLEGE STUDIES

- subjects and opinions
- examinations
- workload
- advantages and disadvantages of homework
- study problems
- the importance of education

SCHOOL/COLLEGE LIFE

Que penses-tu de l'uniforme scolaire ?
What do you think of school uniform?

Je trouve que c'est pratique et assez confortable. C'est une bonne idée, car comme ça on est tous égaux. Par contre, on ne peut pas montrer son individualité. Personnellement, je préfèrerais m'habiller comme je veux !
I think it's practical and quite comfortable. It's a good idea as that way everyone is equal. On the other hand, you can't show your individuality. Personally, I would prefer to dress how I want.

Que fais-tu comme activités extra-scolaires ?
What after-school activities do you do?

En ce moment je ne fais rien car j'ai trop de devoirs mais l'année dernière je faisais de l'athlétisme. Après mes examens je voudrais recommencer ces activités.
At the moment, I don't do anything because I have too much homework but last year I did athletics. After my exams, I'd like to restart these activities.

Comment sont tes professeurs ?
What are your teachers like?

Nous avons de la chance, parce que les professeurs sont très patients et toujours prêts à nous aider. Cependant, il y en a ceux qui sont trop stricts aussi !
We are lucky, because the teachers are very patient and always ready to help us. However, there are also some who are too strict!

Qu'est-ce que tu as fait au collège hier ?
What did you do in school yesterday?

Hier j'ai eu deux examens, donc c'était une journée très longue. J'espère que je vais réussir !
Yesterday I had two exams so it was a very long day. I hope I'm going to pass!

Comment serait ton collège idéal ?
What would your ideal school be like?

Nous n'avons pas de bonnes installations, donc mon collège idéal aurait un terrain de sport et une piscine olympique.
Pour moi, le sport est très important.
We haven't got very good facilities so my ideal school would have a sports ground and an Olympic swimming pool.
Sport is very important to me.

GRAMMAR

Perfect (past) tense with **avoir**

Most verbs are formed in the perfect tense using the present tense of avoir.

Verb endings:

- -er verbs – e.g. étudier → étudié
- -ir verbs – e.g. finir → fini
- -re verbs – e.g. vendre → vendu

To form the perfect tense you first need to add the present tense of avoir.

  J'ai étudié – I studied

Perfect (past) tense with **être**

The following list contains all the verbs that use the present tense of être to form the perfect tense. All reflexive verbs are formed in the same way.

  aller – to go
  arriver – to arrive
  descendre – to go down
  devenir – to become
  entrer – to enter
  monter – to go up
  mourir – to die
  naitre – to be born
  partir – to leave
  rentrer – to go back
  rester – to stay
  retourner – to return
  sortir – to go out
  tomber – to fall
  venir – to come

As they are formed with the present tense of être, the endings of the verbs will need to agree with the subject – e.g. Je suis arrivé(e) – I arrived, nous sommes allé(e)s – we went.

Read this extract from a literary text. Answer the questions in English.

EXAM TASK

Je suis assis à côté de Delphine, c'est le prof de maths qui nous a placés. Les garçons sont assis à côté des filles pour éviter le bavardage. J'ai eu ce prof l'an dernier. Aucun bruit n'est toléré en classe, autrement c'est la porte !

Le prof nous a demandé d'écrire en haut de la page. Nous avons dû marquer notre nom et prénom en lettres majuscules ainsi que le numéro de la classe. Après les maths nous sommes allés au cours d'espagnol et là il y avait du bruit et le prof a dû taper dans les mains pour avoir du silence.

Note: most of the verbs in this extract are in the perfect tense.

1. Where did the writer have to sit and why?
2. Why did the boys have to sit next to the girls?
3. How do we know that the teacher is strict?
4. What did the pupils have to write at the top of the page?
5. What lesson did the pupils have after maths?

Questions on literary texts may be longer and require more thought than the questions at the start of your paper, so make sure you leave enough time to answer them.

SCHOOL/COLLEGE LIFE

Les bâtiments de mon collège sont un peu vieux, mais heureusement nous avons des ressources très modernes.	The buildings in my school are a bit old, but luckily we have very modern resources.
Le règlement de mon collège est assez sévère, mais je suis d'accord avec la plupart des règles.	My school regulations are quite strict but I agree with most of the rules.
J'estime que mon collège est trop strict, parce que les portables sont interdits.	I think my school is too strict because mobile phones are not allowed.
C'est dommage que certains élèves ne respectent pas les professeurs et ne se comportent pas bien.	It's a shame that some pupils don't respect the teachers and don't behave well.
Malheureusement, le harcèlement fait partie de la vie scolaire.	Unfortunately, bullying is part of school life.
Il est extrêmement difficile de résoudre ce problème mais les parents, les élèves et les professeurs doivent travailler ensemble.	It's extremely difficult to solve this problem but parents, pupils and teachers must work together.
De nos jours les examens sont très importants, donc en général il y a une bonne ambiance de travail.	These days exams are important so there is a good work atmosphere.
Les professeures pensent qu'on se comporte mieux quand on porte un uniforme scolaire.	The teachers think you behave better when you wear a school uniform.
Je dirais que l'uniforme scolaire réduit les inégalités entre riches et pauvres.	I would say school uniform reduces inequalities between rich and poor.
Je suis contre l'uniforme scolaire, puisque ce n'est pas à la mode et cela tient trop chaud en été.	I'm against school uniform because it's not fashionable and it makes you too hot in summer.
Les activités extra-scolaires nous permettent d'atteindre un équilibre entre le travail scolaire et les loisirs.	Extracurricular activities allow us to find a balance between school work and leisure.
Pendant la récréation, normalement je bavarde avec mes copains et je mange un snack.	During breaktime, I usually chat with my friends and I eat a snack.
Pendant la pause déjeuner, je mange à la cantine. Il y a beaucoup de choix et les repas sont assez sains – par exemple, il n'y a pas de frites !	During the lunch break, I eat in the canteen. There is a lot of choice and the meals are quite healthy – for example, there are no chips!

You may be asked to describe your school day in your speaking or writing exam. Look at this description:

On commence à neuf heures moins le quart et on finit à trois heures. On a cinq cours par jour et chaque cours dure cinquante-cinq minutes. Il y a une récréation à onze heures et une pause déjeuner à midi et demi.

Try not to give answers like this all the time. This is correct French but it's just a list! There are no opinions, no justifications, no reasons and it's all in one tense. This would be a much better answer:

On commence à neuf heures moins le quart et on finit à trois heures. À mon avis, c'est une journée trop longue. On a cinq cours par jour et chaque cours dure cinquante-cinq minutes. Hier j'ai eu deux cours de maths – c'était ennuyeux ! Il y a une récréation à onze heures et une pause déjeuner à midi et demi. Pendant la récré j'adore bavarder avec mes copains.

Remember:

In your role play you will have to use the present tense as well as at least one other tense. Watch out for 'trigger' words which show you which tense to use – e.g. yesterday and last weekend show you need to use the past tense, and tomorrow and next week show you need to use the future tense.

If there are no trigger words – as in the first two bullet points that follow – then you will need to use the present tense.

- Describe your school.
- Give your opinion of school uniform.
- Say what you did at break time yesterday.
- Say what homework you did last week.
- Say what you will do tomorrow after school.
- Say what subjects you will study next week.

EXAM TASK

SCHOOL/COLLEGE STUDIES

Quelle est ta matière préférée ? Pourquoi ?
What is your favourite subject? Why?

Ma matière préférée en ce moment c'est l'histoire, car le travail est fascinant et le prof est amusant. En plus, mes amis étudient cette matière avec moi et nous avons de la chance parce que le prof ne nous donne pas trop de devoirs.
My favourite subject at the moment is history as the work is fascinating and the teacher is funny. Also, my friends study this subject with me and we are lucky because the teacher doesn't give us too much homework.

Penses-tu que les examens sont importants ?
Do you think exams are important?

Les examens sont indispensables si on veut réussir dans la vie. Je suis complètement obsédé(e) par mes notes et je ne sais pas ce qui va se passer si je ne réussis pas.
Exams are essential if you want to succeed in life. I'm completely obsessed by my grades and I don't know what will happen if I don't pass.

Est-ce que qu'il y a trop de pression au collège ?
Is there too much pressure at school?

Oui, mes parents et mes profs me stressent, tout est stressant ! Si on ne fait pas assez de progrès, on doit travailler plus dur. J'ai trop de contrôles à préparer et on a trop de devoirs.
Yes, my parents and my teachers stress me, everything is stressful! If you don't make enough progress, you have to work harder. I have too many tests to revise for and we have too much homework.

Qu'est-ce que tu as fait comme devoirs le weekend dernier ?
What homework did you do last weekend?

J'ai eu tellement de devoirs le weekend dernier que j'ai dû renoncer à toute activité extra-scolaire. C'était épuisant.
I had so much homework last weekend that I had to give up all my extracurricular activities. It was exhausting.

Qu'est-ce que tu vas étudier l'année prochaine ?
What are you going to study next year?

J'ai toujours de bonnes notes en sciences et j'adore faire des expériences donc je vais continuer avec la biologie, mais je dois choisir entre la chimie et la physique. Je vais laisser tomber la géographie, car je ne m'intéresse pas du tout à cette matière.
I've always had good grades in science and I love doing experiments so I am going to continue with biology, but I must choose between chemistry and physics. I'm going to drop geography as I'm not interested in that subject at all.

You are likely to have at least one multiple-choice question in your reading and/or listening exam.
The question may be in English or French or use pictures. Top tips:

- Don't answer too soon! Make sure you read **all** of the options before choosing your answer and don't just stop when you come to the one that seems most likely.

- Some of the answers may be deliberately trying to trick you! Several alternatives may seem correct, so it is important to read the text and the questions carefully.

- If you are not sure of an answer, guess … but do so methodically. Eliminate some choices you know are wrong. Try to narrow down the answer to one or two alternatives and then compare them. Finally, make an informed decision.

EXAM TASK

Now practise your multiple-choice strategies on this task.

Choisis la bonne réponse.

Nous avons deux types de classes – monolingue (ça veut dire que tous les cours sont en français) et bilingue (la moitié des cours sont en français et l'autre moitié en breton). Ce sont les familles qui choisissent. Aujourd'hui par exemple, les enfants ont les maths et le français le matin en langue française. Et l'après-midi, on enseigne l'histoire-géo en breton.

On fait aussi la gymnastique en breton et en français. Cette année nous avons cinquante élèves qui suivent les cours en classes bilingues et trente-huit élèves qui suivent les cours seulement en français.

1. Il y a combien de sortes de classes ?
   a. 2
   b. 8
   c. 10
2. Dans une classe monolingue, on parle…
   a. le breton et l'anglais
   b. le français
   c. le breton et le français
3. Dans une classe bilingue, on parle…
   a. le breton et l'anglais
   b. le français
   c. le breton et le français
4. Qui fait le choix de la classe ?
   a. Le professeur
   b. L'élève
   c. Les parents et l'élève
5. Le matin on étudie…
   a. les maths et l'histoire
   b. les maths et le français
   c. le français et le breton
6. Comme sport on fait…
   a. du judo
   b. de la danse
   c. de la gymnastique
7. Il y combien d'élèves dans les classes bilingues ?
   a. 15
   b. 38
   c. 50

SCHOOL/COLLEGE STUDIES

Je suis bon(ne) élève et maintenant j'essaie toujours de réussir.	I'm a good student and now I always try to succeed.
Le prof explique tout très bien et les cours sont toujours stimulants.	The teacher explains well and the lessons are always stimulating.
Je m'ennuie pendant les cours et le prof nous donne trop de devoirs.	I get bored in the lessons and the teacher gives us too much homework.
Franchement je suis nul(le) en anglais et les cours ne sont jamais intéressants.	Frankly I'm rubbish at English and the lessons are never interesting.
Cette matière (ne) sera (pas) utile pour moi à l'avenir.	This subject will (not) be useful for me in the future.
Je suis fort(e) en musique et je me passionne pour cette matière.	I'm good at music and I'm passionate about this subject.
Je suis faible en dessin, donc le prof me donne toujours de mauvaises notes.	I'm not good at art so the teacher always gives me bad marks.
J'ai toujours adoré les maths, car j'aime faire des calculs.	I've always loved maths, as I like doing calculations.
Certaines matières sont essentielles pour trouver un bon travail – par exemple, les langues.	Certain subjects are essential for finding a good job – for example, languages.
J'ai du mal à me concentrer en classe.	I find it hard to concentrate in class.
Si j'avais su l'importance de la préparation pour les examens, j'aurais commencé plus tôt.	If I had known the importance of exam preparation, I would have started earlier.
J'ai peur de décevoir mes parents.	I'm scared of disappointing my parents.
Le stress des examens m'empêche de dormir et de manger normalement.	Exam stress prevents me from sleeping and eating normally.
La première cause de stress chez les jeunes semble être les études.	The main cause of stress among young people seems to be studies.
Il faut établir un programme de révisions pour éviter le stress.	You have to establish a revision programme to avoid stress.
L'année dernière, je détestais mes profs parce qu'ils étaient stricts et ennuyeux.	Last year I hated my teachers because they were strict and boring.
À l'école primaire, les profs étaient très attentifs et rendaient les cours amusants.	At primary school, my teachers were very helpful and made lessons fun.
Avant, j'étudiais la chimie mais c'était trop difficile.	Before, I used to study chemistry but it was too difficult.

Remember that you will be marked for accuracy at both Foundation and Higher level. Carefully check spellings, accents, genders, plurals and tenses.

Remember to include additional tenses, if possible, to show off your grammatical knowledge. In this task, for example, you are asked to write about your primary school (past tense) and your plans for September (future tense). Then why not try to talk about your ideal school or what you would like to do in the future as well (conditional tense)?

As with the conversation part of the speaking exam, this is your opportunity to show what you can do. If you're not quite sure how to say something, write it another way – it doesn't have to be true as long as it makes sense!

You are in control in this exam but don't just write what you want – make sure you answer the question and spend equal time on all three bullet points!

EXAM TASK

Écris un article pour le site web de ton collège. Écris au sujet de :
- Ton école primaire (passé)
- Ton collège (présent)
- Ce que tu vas faire en septembre comme matières

CURRENT AND FUTURE STUDY AND EMPLOYMENT

ENTERPRISE, EMPLOYABILITY AND FUTURE PLANS

The sub-theme of **Enterprise, Employability and Future Plans** is divided into four areas. Here are some suggestions of topics to revise:

EMPLOYMENT

- advantages and disadvantages of employment and work experience
- saving money
- pocket money
- voluntary work
- part-time jobs
- how you spend the money you earn

SKILLS AND PERSONAL QUALITIES

- personality traits
- personal skills
- skills for different jobs
- application letters
- job interviews

POST-16 STUDY

- job and college applications
- formal letters
- CVs
- interviews – e.g. for work, college and university
- job and course adverts

CAREER PLANS

- training and study options
- job opportunities
- working abroad
- future plans
- interviews at an employment agency

EMPLOYMENT

Que fais-tu pour gagner de l'argent ?
What do you do to earn money?

Avant je travaillais dans un magasin et c'était un travail assez bien payé, mais maintenant j'ai trop de travail scolaire. J'ai de la chance, parce que mes parents me donnent de l'argent de poche chaque semaine si j'aide à la maison.
Before, I used to work in a shop and it was quite a well-paid job but now I have too much school work. I am lucky because my parents give me pocket money every week if I help at home.

Est-ce qu'il est important de travailler pendant les vacances scolaires ?
Is it important to work in the school holidays?

En général, je pense que c'est une bonne idée pour les jeunes de travailler pendant les vacances. Ça donne aux jeunes l'occasion d'apprendre de nouvelles choses et de gagner de l'argent.
In general, I think it's a good idea for young people to work in the holidays. It gives young people the opportunity to learn new things and earn money.

Quels sont les aspects négatifs d'un petit boulot ?
What are the negative aspects of having a part-time/casual job?

Mes copains me disent que leurs petits boulots ne sont pas bien payés. Le travail peut être monotone et on n'a pas assez de temps pour faire le travail scolaire.
My friends tell me that their part-time/casual jobs are not well paid. The work can be monotonous and you haven't got enough time to do school work.

Qu'est-ce que tu aimerais faire comme travail pendant les vacances ?
What would you like to do as a holiday job?

J'aimerais travailler en plein air comme moniteur/monitrice de natation. Ça me permettrait d'aider les autres et je pense que le travail serait varié.
I would like to work outdoors as a swimming instructor. That would allow me to help other people and I think the job would be varied.

Est-ce que tu as fait un stage ?
Have you done work experience?

Non, je n'ai jamais travaillé et je n'ai pas eu l'occasion de faire un stage en entreprise. Un jour je voudrais devenir journaliste, donc je devrais faire un stage dans le bureau du journal régional.
No, I have never worked and I haven't had the opportunity to do work experience. One day I would like to be a journalist, so I should do a work placement in the office of the regional newspaper.

The perfect infinitive is formed by using the infinitive of **avoir** or the infinitive of **être** plus the past participle of the verb. It means 'to have done'.

It is most often used with the phrase **après avoir** or **après être** (after having done …) – e.g. **Après avoir** fini le travail, nous sommes allés manger au restaurant. (After having finished work, we went to eat in the restaurant.)

Remember, when using **être** in the perfect tense there will need to be agreement with the past participle – e.g. Après être arrivé(e) au travail, j'ai bu un café. (After arriving at work, I drank a coffee.)

GRAMMAR

Write a suitable ending for these sentences.
1. Après avoir fait un stage, _____ .
2. Après être allé(e) au travail, _____ .
3. Après avoir trouvé un emploi, _____ .
4. Après avoir parlé avec le patron, _____ .

EXAM TASK

Answer the questions in English.
Mylène : Je suis allée à Londres pour travailler comme au pair avec une famille. J'ai amélioré mon anglais et en même temps j'ai gagné de l'argent de poche.

Sylvie : Je suis restée chez moi. Je garde des animaux pour les voisins quand ils sont en vacances. J'aime bien promener les chiens.

Alain : Moi, je suis moniteur dans un club de vacances. Je m'occupe des enfants et je suis moniteur de voile aussi. Cela me permet d'avoir de l'expérience et de l'argent.

1. Why did Mylène go to London? Which **two** benefits does she mention?
2. How does Sylvie earn money? How do we know she likes her job?
3. Which **two** activities does Alain do?

EMPLOYMENT

Je pense que faire un stage en entreprise est une bonne préparation pour la vie.

I think that doing a work placement is good preparation for life.

Si on veut trouver un bon travail un jour, ce sera nécessaire de faire un stage.

If you want to find a good job one day, it wil be necessary to do work experience.

Il faut travailler dur à l'école pour réussir aux exams, donc je n'ai pas assez de temps pour faire un petit boulot.

You have to work hard at school to pass exams, so I haven't got enough time to have a part-time/ casual job.

J'ai beaucoup apprécié mon stage et j'ai appris beaucoup de choses.

I really appreciated my work experience and I learned a lot of things.

On me donnait des choses intéressantes à faire et je m'entendais bien avec mon patron.

They gave me interesting things to do and I got on well with my boss.

Avant, les élèves de mon collège faisaient un stage en entreprise, mais maintenant ce n'est pas possible.

Before, pupils in my school used to do work experience but now it's not possible.

Je voudrais trouver un petit boulot qui me permettra d'utiliser mes langues étrangères.

I'd like to find a part-time/casual job that will allow me to use my foreign languages.

J'ai de la chance, parce que je rencontre beaucoup de gens au travail et je ne m'ennuie jamais.

I'm lucky, because I meet lots of people at work and I never get bored.

Je pense qu'un stage permet aux jeunes de mieux connaitre un métier particulier.

I think work experience allows young people to get to know a particular job better.

J'ai des économies grâce à l'argent reçu pour mon anniversaire.

I have some savings thanks to money from my birthday.

Je réfléchis toujours avant de dépenser mon argent.

I always think before spending my money.

Je dépense mon argent dès que je le reçois et je ne fais jamais d'économies.

I spend my money as soon as I receive it and I never save.

Je peux acheter des choses que mes parents ne veulent pas me payer.

I can buy things that my parents don't want to pay for.

L'argent de poche me donne une certaine indépendance, car il me permet d'acheter ce que je veux.

Pocket money gives me some independence as it allows me to buy what I want.

L'argent que je gagne me rend plus indépendant(e) et me permet d'apprendre la valeur des choses.

The money I earn makes me more independent and allows me to learn the value of things.

Si je trouvais un petit boulot et je gagnais de l'argent, j'apprendrais à devenir plus responsable.

If I found a part-time/casual job and earned money, I would learn to be more responsible.

Expressing opinions:

Pour moi/À mon avis/Selon moi/Pour ma part – In my opinion
Je pense que/Je crois que – I think that
Je trouve que – I find that
Il semble que – It seems that

EXAM TASK

Answer these questions in French.

- Décris cette photo. (Foundation)/Qu'est-ce qui se passe sur cette photo ? (Higher)
  Describe the photo./What is happening in the photo?
- Est-ce qu'il est important de gagner de l'argent ? Pourquoi (pas) ? Is it important to
  earn money? Why (not)?
- Les jeunes ont besoin d'avoir de l'expérience du monde du travail. Qu'en penses-tu ?
  Young people need experience of the world of work. What do you think?
- Est-ce que tu aimerais un petit boulot ? Pourquoi (pas) ? Would you like a part-time/
  casual job? Why (not)?

Useful phrases for describing a picture:

sur l'image – in the picture
je vois – I see
il y a – there is
on peut voir – one can see
ça montre – it shows
à l'arrière-plan – in the background
au premier plan – in the foreground

SKILLS AND PERSONAL QUALITIES

Quelles sont tes qualités personnelles ?
What are your personal qualities?

Je suis tout le temps souriant(e) et accueillant(e), et je sais mettre les gens à l'aise. Je me considère extraverti(e) puisque je j'exprime facilement mes opinions devant les autres.
I am always smiling and welcoming, and I know how to put people at ease. I consider myself to be an extrovert as I express my opinions in front of others easily.

Quelles sont tes compétences pour le monde du travail ?
What skills do you have for the world of work?

À mon avis, je travaille bien en équipe parce que je m'entends bien avec tout le monde. Par ailleurs, je peux être un leader quand la situation l'exige.
In my opinion, I work well in a team because I get on well with everyone. Furthermore, I can be a leader when the situation demands.

Quelles sont les compétences nécessaires pour trouver un bon travail ?
What are the skills needed to find a good job?

Si on veut trouver un bon emploi, il vaut mieux parler une langue étrangère. Pour réussir de nos jours, il faut avoir l'esprit d'initiative et prendre des risques.
If you want to find a good job, it's best to speak a foreign language. To succeed these days, you need to show initiative and to take risks.

Comment serait ton/ta patron(ne) idéal(e) ?
What would your ideal boss be like?

Mon/ma patron(ne) idéal(e) créerait un esprit d'équipe et un milieu de travail positif. Il/elle serait ouvert(e) au changement et il/elle écouterait les idées de ses employés.
My ideal boss would create a team spirit and a positive workplace. He/she would be open to change and he or she would listen to the ideas of his/her employees.

Décris ta plus grande réussite au collège.
Describe your biggest success at school.

Ma plus grande fierté au collège c'était quand j'ai réussi tous mes examens l'année dernière. J'ai reçu de très bonnes notes.
My proudest moment at school was when I passed all my exams last year. I got really good grades.

When you are talking about your skills and personal qualities you will often need to give examples to illustrate the points you are making.
Here are some useful expressions in French:

par exemple – for example
comme – like
tel(s)/telle(s) que – such as
quant à – regarding
en ce qui concerne... – as far as ... is concerned
prenons... comme exemple – let's take ... as an example
il est évident que – it is obvious that

EXAM TASK

Match 1–10 to a–j.

1. travailler régulièrement
2. communiquer avec les autres
3. inventer et créer
4. aider les autres
5. être en bonne santé
6. travailler manuellement
7. travailler dehors
8. être responsable
9. utiliser la technologie
10. parler des langues étrangères

a. to be in good health
b. to use technology
c. to work regularly
d. to work with your hands
e. to be responsible
f. to speak foreign languages
g. to work outside
h. to invent and create
i. to communicate with others
j. to help others

SKILLS AND PERSONAL QUALITIES

Je m'adapte facilement aux nouvelles situations. — I adapt easily to new situations.

J'ai d'excellentes aptitudes à la communication. — I have excellent communication skills.

J'ai suivi une bonne formation, mais je suis toujours disposé(e) à apprendre. — I have had good training but I am always ready to learn.

Je n'ai pas peur de poser des questions si je ne comprends pas quelque chose. — I'm not scared of asking questions if I don't understand something.

Je suis très organisé(e) et je gère bien le stress. — I am very organised and I manage stress well.

J'ai besoin d'améliorer mes connaissances techniques. — I need to improve my technical knowledge.

J'aimerais perfectionner mes compétences linguistiques. — I would like to perfect my language skills.

Je sais lire entre les lignes et identifier les problèmes. — I can read between the lines and I can identify problems.

J'accepte toujours les critiques constructives. — I always accept constructive criticism.

Mes qualités personnelles me permettront de répondre aux défis du monde du travail. — My personal qualities will allow me to respond to the challenges of the world of work.

J'ai déjà appris des compétences professionnelles grâce à mes études de commerce au collège. — I have already learned professional skills thanks to my study of business at school.

Tout travailleur doit démontrer sa capacité à apprendre et à évoluer. — Every worker must show their ability to learn and to evolve.

Dans notre environnement globalisé, il faut que les gens soient ouverts au changement. — In our global environment, people must be open to change.

Avec la technologie en constante évolution, il faut être capable de s'adapter rapidement à des situations variées. — With the constant evolution of technology, you must be able to adapt quickly to different situations.

Il faut savoir écouter et accepter les idées des autres. — You need to know how to listen and accept the ideas of other people.

Je peux exécuter plusieurs tâches à la fois. — I can multitask.

J'ai toujours été très motivé(e). — I have always been very motivated.

Quand j'étais petit(e), je n'étais pas une personne ambitieuse. — When I was younger, I wasn't an ambitious person.

 You will need to use appropriate language to emphasise a point you are making.

Here are some helpful expressions in French:

par-dessus tout – above all
surtout – especially
particulièrement – particularly
en particulier – in particular
en effet – indeed
d'ailleurs – furthermore
en fait – in fact

Write one full sentence in French for each job.

- doctor
- teacher
- pilot
- police officer
- secretary
- IT technician

Look at the exam task on page 95. Try to use some of the vocabulary to help you here.

POST-16 STUDY

Est-ce que tu veux continuer tes études l'année prochaine ?
Do you want to continue your studies next year?

À mon avis, la vie scolaire est stressante mais j'ai l'intention de trouver un bon travail à l'avenir, donc je continuerai mes études l'année prochaine. Je vais étudier l'anglais, l'histoire et le français.
In my opinion, school life is stressful but I intend to find a good job in the future, so I will continue with my studies next year. I am going to study English, history and French.

Aimerais-tu aller à l'université ? Pourquoi (pas) ?
Would you like to go to university? Why (not)?

Quand j'étais petit(e), c'était mon rêve d'aller à l'université pour devenir avocat(e), mais maintenant j'ai changé d'avis. Je pense que la formation serait trop longue et ennuyeuse et couterait trop cher.
When I was younger, it was my dream to go to university to become a lawyer, but now I have changed my mind. I think that the training would be too long and boring and it would be too expensive.

Est-ce qu'il est essentiel pour les jeunes d'aller à l'université ?
Is it essential for young people to go to university?

Bien sûr, les diplômes peuvent nous aider dans le monde du travail, mais ils ne sont pas le seul moyen de réussir. Pour avoir du succès dans la vie, il faut plutôt être travailleur et ambitieux.
Of course, degrees can help us in the world of work but they are not the only way of being successful. To be successful in life, you really need to be hard-working and ambitious.

Quels sont les avantages d'une année sabbatique ?
What are the advantages of a gap year?

Je pense qu'une année sabbatique est un moyen formidable d'enrichir sa vie. Par exemple, on pourrait apprendre une nouvelle langue ou voyager et explorer le monde.
I think a gap year is an amazing way to enrich your life. For example, you could learn a new language or travel and explore the world.

La vie étudiante coute-t-elle trop cher ? Pourquoi (pas) ?
Is student life too expensive? Why (not)?

Il est vrai que faire des études coute de plus en plus cher, et je ne sais pas si ça vaut vraiment la peine. Mes parents souhaitent que je fasse des études supérieures mais je préfèrerais trouver un bon travail.
It's true that studying is more and more expensive, and I don't know if it's really worth it. My parents want me to continue to higher education but I would prefer to find a good job.

In this unit you may need to understand and use persuasive language and you will also want to ask questions.
Here are a few useful phrases in French:

Expressing hope
J'espère que... – I hope that ...
Je l'espère bien – I really hope so

Seeking/giving information
Pourriez-vous me dire... ? – Could you tell me ...?
Y a-t-il... ? – Is there ...?
À quelle heure... ? – At what time ...?

Expressing intention
Je vais + **infinitive** – I am going to ...
J'ai l'intention de... – I intend to ...

Expressing interest
Je m'intéresse beaucoup à... – I am very interested in ...
Je me passionne pour... – I am passionate about ...

EXAM TASK

Translate the following sentences into English:

1. Je ne sais pas exactement ce que je vais étudier l'année prochaine.
2. À mon avis, les sciences et les langues sont vraiment importantes dans la vie.
3. La chimie et les maths sont des matières qui vont assez bien ensemble.
4. Malheureusement, il va falloir que je travaille très dur.
5. Si j'ai de bonnes notes, je continuerai mes études de commerce.

Watch out for intensifiers – e.g. exactement (exactly), **vraiment** (really), **très** (very), **assez** (quite) – and make sure you translate them.

POST-16 STUDY

Pour moi, le choix de poursuivre mon éducation n'était pas difficile.	For me, the decision to continue with my education wasn't difficult.
Pour la grande majorité des jeunes, les études coutent trop cher.	For the vast majority of young people, studies are too expensive.
Je préférerais quitter le collège pour devenir entrepreneur/se.	I would prefer to leave school to become an entrepreneur.
Mes parents sont convaincus que l'enseignement supérieur augmente les chances de réussite.	My parents are convinced that higher education improves your chances of success.
Peut-être que j'irai étudier à l'étranger.	Perhaps I will go to study abroad.
Je vais quitter le collège et travailler pour gagner un peu d'argent.	I'm going to leave school and work to earn some money.
Je voudrais prendre une année sabbatique.	I would like to take a gap year.
Je ne veux pas me lancer tout de suite dans le monde du travail.	I don't want to throw myself into the world of work immediately.
Je voudrais continuer mes études, mais je ne sais pas où.	I would like to continue my studies, but I don't know where.
On nous dit qu'avoir un diplôme est essentiel pour survivre dans l'économie actuelle.	We've been told that having a degree is essential to survive in the current economy.
Il faut avouer qu'il y a des milliers de gens qui gagnent bien leur vie sans être diplômés.	You must admit that there are thousands of people who earn a good living without having a degree.
Cependant, il n'est pas toujours nécessaire de poursuivre des études pour trouver un emploi.	However, it isn't always necessary to continue your studies to find a job.
Le cout d'un diplôme est devenu un argument contre l'enseignement supérieur.	The cost of a degree has become an argument against higher education.
Beaucoup de professions n'ont pas besoin d'un diplôme.	Many professions don't need a degree.
Je voudrais passer mes examens et réussir dans la vie.	I want to sit my exams and succeed in life.
Je n'ai pas l'intention de rester au lycée et j'espère faire une formation professionnelle.	I don't intend to stay at sixth form and I hope to do a professional training course.
J'espère réussir à mes examens.	I hope to pass my exams.
Si je ne réussis pas à mes examens, je ferai un apprentissage.	If I don't pass my exams, I will do an apprenticeship.

In the speaking exam, don't worry if you don't understand the question at first. You won't lose marks if you ask your teacher to repeat what they said.

Here are some useful phrases in French:

- Je n'ai pas compris. I didn't understand.
- Je ne comprends pas. I don't understand.
- Peux-tu répéter s'il te plait ? Can you please repeat? (informal)
- Pouvez-vous répéter s'il vous plait ? Can you please repeat? (formal)
- Qu'est-ce que ça veut dire ? What does that mean?
- Pardon ? Sorry/Pardon?
- Je suis désolé(e). I'm sorry.
- Pardon, qu'est-ce que tu as dit ? Sorry, what did you say? (informal)
- Pardon, qu'est-ce que vous avez dit ? Sorry, what did you say? (formal)

EXAM TASK

Here are some examples of conversation questions:

- Est-ce que tu veux continuer tes études l'année prochaine ? Pourquoi (pas) ? Do you want to continue your studies next year? Why (not)?
- Que veux-tu faire comme travail plus tard dans la vie ? What do you want to do as a job later in life?
- Est-ce que tu veux aller à l'université ? Pourquoi (pas) ? Do you want to go to university? Why (not)?
- Pourquoi as-tu choisi ces matières ? Why did you choose your subjects?
- Les écoles préparent les jeunes pour le travail. Qu'en penses-tu ? School prepares young people for work. What do you think?
- Quelles sont tes compétences pour le travail ? What workplace skills do you have?

CAREER PLANS

Que veux-tu faire plus tard dans la vie ?
What do you want to do later in life?

Si je réussis à mes examens, j'ai l'intention d'aller à l'université. Après mes études j'aimerais trouver un travail intéressant et je veux gagner beaucoup d'argent !
If I pass my exams, I intend to go to university. After my studies, I would like to find an interesting job and I want to earn lots of money!

Est-ce qu'il est difficile pour les jeunes de trouver un bon emploi ? Pourquoi (pas) ?
Is it hard for young people to find a good job? Why (not)?

Je ne sais pas pourquoi il est si difficile de trouver un emploi actuellement. Il y a beaucoup de chômage et j'imagine qu'il n'y a pas assez d'emplois pour les jeunes.
I don't know why it's so hard to find a job currently. There is lots of unemployment and I imagine there are not enough jobs for young people.

Aimerais-tu travailler à l'étranger ? Pourquoi (pas) ?
Would you like to work abroad? Why (not)?

Selon moi, travailler à l'étranger est une bonne idée parce qu'on peut développer de nouvelles compétences. Personnellement, j'aimerais travailler aux États-Unis parce qu'il y a de nombreuses opportunités là-bas.
In my opinion, working abroad is a good idea because you can develop new skills. Personally, I would like to work in the United States because there are lots of opportunities there.

Que feras-tu dans dix ans ?
What will you do in ten years?

J'espère que dans dix ans je serai content(e) et riche ! J'aurai fini mes études et je ferai un travail très bien payé et satisfaisant. J'habiterai dans une grande maison avec une piscine et j'aimerais me marier et avoir des enfants aussi.
I hope that in ten years I will be happy and rich! I will have finished my studies and I will have a very well-paid and satisfying job. I will live in a big house with a swimming pool I would like to get married and have children too.

Que voulais-tu faire quand tu étais petit(e) ?
What did you want to do when you were younger?

Quand j'étais plus jeune, je rêvais d'être chanteur/chanteuse parce que je voulais être célèbre. Maintenant je n'ai aucune envie d'être célèbre – ça ne m'intéresse pas du tout !
When I was younger I dreamt of being a singer because I wanted to be famous. Now I don't have any desire to be famous – it doesn't interest me at all!

Here are some helpful phrases to use when discussing your future:

après avoir/être + **past participle** – after having done something
avant de + **infinitive** – before doing something
tout d'abord – first of all
premièrement – firstly
deuxièmement – secondly
plus tard – later
pendant que – while

GRAMMAR

Future plans

Write a paragraph about your future plans. Use all of the time phrases on the left to sequence your paragraph and use all of the structures on the right at least once each. You can use them in any order. Don't forget to include the future tense in your paragraph as well.

à l'avenir...	vouloir + **infinitive**
après mes examens...	espérer + **infinitive**
dans dix ans...	avoir l'intention de +
premièrement...	**infinitive**
plus tard...	aller + **infinitive**

Answer the questions.

EXAM TASK

Annie : L'année prochaine, j'étudierai quatre matières. Je sais que je vais poursuivre[1] mes études en biologie et en chimie, mais pour les autres je n'ai pas encore décidé.

Germaine : Si j'obtiens de bonnes notes, j'irai à l'université. Je vais prendre une année sabbatique[2] avant d'aller à l'université.

Hervé : Les voyages me passionnent et j'ai de la chance[3] parce que l'année prochaine j'irai rendre visite à ma famille en Thaïlande avant de travailler comme cuisinier.

Régis : À l'avenir je vais continuer d'étudier les langues à l'université. Je voudrais étudier l'espagnol et l'italien.

Thierry : Je voudrais aller à l'université de Lyon, mais cela dépendra[4] de mes résultats.

Paul : Je chercherai un travail bien payé, car à mon avis le salaire est très important.

1 continue
2 gap year
3 I'm lucky
4 that will depend

Who ...

1. will take a gap year?
2. will work as a cook?
3. wants to study languages?
4. will be studying more than three subjects?
5. thinks money is important?
6. plans to travel?

CAREER PLANS

Quand je finis mes études, je chercherai un bon emploi avec un salaire élevé.	When I finish my studies, I will look for a good job with a high salary.
Je préfèrerais travailler à mon compte et gagner beaucoup d'argent.	I would prefer to work for myself and earn lots of money.
Je voudrais obtenir un bon diplôme et je rêve d'être avocat(e).	I want to be well-qualified and I dream of being a lawyer.
Je vais économiser pour acheter une maison.	I am going to save to buy a house.
J'ai toujours rêvé d'être professeur parce que le travail m'inspire.	I've always dreamt of being a teacher as the work inspires me.
J'espère trouver un emploi près/loin de chez moi.	I hope to find a job near to/far from where I live.
Il faut admettre que je n'ai aucune idée de ce que je voudrais faire.	I must admit I don't have any idea what I would like to do.
Je n'ai pas encore décidé quelle carrière je veux faire plus tard dans la vie.	I haven't yet decided what career I want to do later in life.
Comme tout le monde, je ne veux pas être au chômage.	Like everyone, I don't want to be unemployed.
Je ne veux pas avoir un travail monotone.	I don't want to have a monotonous job.
Je veux poursuivre une carrière passionnante.	I want to pursue an exciting career.
Après mes études, je voudrais habiter en Australie.	After my studies, I would like to live in Australia.
J'espère travailler à l'étranger pour améliorer mes compétences linguistiques.	I hope to work abroad to improve my language skills.
Un jour je voudrais faire le tour du monde.	One day I would like to travel the world.
Quand j'avais dix ans, je rêvais de devenir astronaute.	When I was ten, I dreamt of becoming an astronaut.

You may need to read or write a letter of application for this unit. Here are some useful phrases:

- Ayant lu votre annonce dans le journal au sujet du poste de... – Having seen your newspaper advert for the job of …
- J'ai déjà eu des expériences de... – I have already had experience of …
- Je voudrais travailler parce que... – I would like to work because …
- Je m'intéresse surtout à ce poste. – I am especially interested in this job.
- Vous trouverez ci-joint mon CV. – You will find attached my CV.

If you can use these phrases in your exam they will show off your ability to use different tenses.

EXAM TASK

Translate the following into French:
Would you like to work abroad?

Yes, perhaps I will spend a year in France as a secretary in an office. I don't want to be an IT technician but I like working with computers. I really need to improve my language skills. Last year I went to Spain and didn't understand anything!

GRAMMAR

GRAMMAR TERMS

It's important to understand what these terms mean as they will be used regularly throughout your GCSE course.

Adjectives: Adjectives describe nouns. They answer the questions: which, what kind of, how many – e.g. grand (big), petit (little), intéressant (interesting).

Adverbs: Adverbs describe verbs (and sometimes adjectives and other adverbs). They answer the questions: how, when, where – e.g. régulièrement (regularly).

Articles: These include the definite article – le/la/l'/les (the) – and the indefinite article – un/une (a/an).

Comparative: This is a form of adjective or adverb. It's used when comparing two things – e.g. meilleur (better).

Connective/Conjunction: This is a word or phrase that connects two ideas or parts of a sentence – e.g. parce que (because).

Demonstratives: These are words which demonstrate (point out) – e.g. ce, cette (this, that, these, those).

Gender: Used for nouns to say if they're masculine or feminine.

Imperative: A form of a verb used when giving instructions or commands – e.g. donnez !

Infinitive: This is the form of verb you find in the dictionary. In English it always has the word 'to' in front of it – e.g. 'to study' – and in French it ends in -er, -ir or -re.

Irregular verb: A verb that does not follow regular patterns and has a different form when conjugated. These usually need to be learned by heart – e.g. aller (to go).

Noun: A person, place, thing or idea.

Object: The object is the person/thing in a sentence which has the action happen to it.

Plural: More than one of an item.

Possessives: These are words that imply ownership – e.g. ma maison (my house).

Prepositions: These are words which help describe something's location or give other information – e.g. dans (in), sur (on).

Pronouns: These are words which take the place of nouns in a sentence.

Reflexive verbs: Reflexive verbs have their action done to the person who is doing the action) – e.g. se coucher (to go to sleep).

Singular: Refers to only one of an item (as opposed to plural for more than one).

Subject: The person or thing in the sentence that is doing the action.

Superlative: The superlative is *the most* of something – e.g. le mieux (the best), le pire (the worst), le plus grand (the biggest).

Synonyms: Words which share the same meaning are synonyms.

Tense: This is a change in the verb to describe actions happening in the past, present, future or conditional.

Verbs: These are the action words which are doing something in a sentence.

Don't panic when you see the following grammar list! This is a list of **every** grammar point that might come up at GCSE. You won't need to use all of these grammar points yourself, but it will help if you are able to recognise different linguistic features. This reference section means that you can look up any grammar terms that are confusing you. There are also some grammar exercises throughout so that you can practise your knowledge. The verb tables at the back of this section will be useful when you are revising for your speaking and writing exams.

NOUNS

MASCULINE AND FEMININE

Nouns are words for things, people and ideas. In French, all nouns are either masculine or feminine –
e.g. **le livre** (the book), **la table** (the table).

PLURALS

To make nouns plural you usually:

- Add -s to nouns ending in a vowel – e.g. livre → livre**s**
- Change the ending -al to -aux – e.g. animal → anim**aux**
- Change the ending -ou to -oux – e.g. bijou → bij**oux**
- Change the ending -eau to -eaux – e.g. chapeau → chap**eaux**
- Change the ending -eu to -eux – e.g. feu → f**eux**

There are some plurals which don't follow the rule – e.g.:

> l'œil → les yeux
> le nez → les nez
> l'os → les os
> le prix → les prix
> le temps → les temps

ARTICLES

DEFINITE ARTICLES (LE/LA/L'/LES)

In French, the word for 'the' changes depending on whether the noun it goes with is masculine, feminine or plural – e.g. le garçon → les garçons, la maison → les maisons.

The definite articles (le, la, l', les (the)) are used more often in French than in English – e.g. Je déteste le poulet. (I hate chicken.)

When using the preposition à, the forms are: au/à la/à l'/aux, depending on the gender of the noun – e.g. **à la** gare (at the train station), **au** cinéma (at the cinema).

When using the preposition de, the forms are: du/de la/de l'/des – e.g. **des** baguettes.

INDEFINITE ARTICLES (UN/UNE/DES)

Indefinite articles (un/une/des (a/an/some)) are left out when stating people's jobs – e.g. Mon père est technicien. (My father is a technician.)

ADJECTIVES

MAKING ADJECTIVES AGREE WITH THE NOUN

In French, all adjectives (words that describe people, places and things) have different endings depending on whether the noun they are describing is masculine, feminine or plural. In other words, adjectives always have to *agree* with the noun – e.g. joli/jolie/jolis/jolies.

Normally an adjective is made feminine by adding **-e**. If the word already ends in an 'e' it does not change – e.g. jeune.

Many adjectives have irregular feminine forms. Here are some that you may come across (these are the singular forms):

Masculine	Feminine	English
ancien	ancienne	old
bas	basse	low
beau	belle	beautiful
blanc	blanche	white
bon	bonne	good
cher	chère	dear
doux	douce	sweet
faux	fausse	false
favori	favorite	favourite
fou	folle	mad
frais	fraiche	fresh
gentil	gentille	kind
gras	grasse	fat
gros	grosse	big
jaloux	jalouse	jealous
long	longue	long
nouveau	nouvelle	new
premier	première	first
public	publique	public
sec	sèche	dry
vieux	vieille	old

Some adjectives that are used before a masculine singular noun beginning with a vowel or an 'h' also change. The most common are un **bel** homme (a handsome man) and un **nouvel** ordinateur (a new computer).

To make a masculine or feminine adjective plural, add -s on to the end of the adjective – e.g. mes prop**res** vêtements (my own clothes).

For adjectives ending in -au, add -x instead of -s – e.g. nouveau → nouveaux. Most adjectives ending in -al change to -aux in the plural – e.g. principal → princip**aux**.

POSITION OF ADJECTIVES

Most adjectives in French go after the noun they are describing – e.g. la voiture **blanche**, le garçon **intelligent**.

The following adjectives go before the noun: beau, bon, excellent, gentil, grand, gros, jeune, joli, long, mauvais, même, meilleur, nouveau, petit, vieux, vilain.

Some adjectives change their meaning depending on whether they come before or after the noun. These are the most common:

> un cher ami – a dear friend
> un portable cher – an expensive mobile phone
> un ancien ami – a former friend
> un bâtiment ancien – an old building
> ma propre chamber – my own bedroom
> ma chambre propre – my clean bedroom

COMPARATIVES AND SUPERLATIVES

You use comparative adjectives to compare two things and say one is bigger, smaller, better, etc. than the other. Superlative adjectives are used to compare two things and say which one is the best, worst, biggest, etc.

To form the comparative and superlative of adjectives which go before the noun, the following pattern is used:

plus (more)	moins (less)	aussi (as)
le/la/les plus (the most)	le/la/les moins (the least)	-
plus fort (stronger)*	moins fort (less strong)*	aussi fort (as strong)*
the strongest: le plus fort la plus forte les plus fort(e)s	the least strong: le moins fort la moins forte les moins fort(e)s	-

* In these three cases que is used to make a comparison – e.g.:

- Arnaud est plus fort **que** Philippe. Arnaud is stronger than Philippe.
- Les lions sont aussi forts **que** les tigres. Lions are as strong as tigers.

Adjectives which go after a noun take the following pattern:

- Une émission plus amusante. A more interesting programme. (comparative)
- L'émission la plus amusante. The most interesting programme. (superlative)

Note the repetition of l' and la in the superlative form.

The same patterns can be applied to adverbs.

- Elle court plus vite que moi. She runs faster than me. (comparative adverb)
- C'est elle qui court le plus vite. She is the one who runs the fastest. (superlative adverb)

GRAMMAR

Choose the correct adjective and then translate each sentence into English.

1. Une voiture est plus **chère/chers/cher** qu'un vélo.
2. Les avions sont les plus **impressionnant/impressionnantes/impressionnants**.
3. Un livre est moins **intéressante/intéressant/intéressants** qu'une tablette.
4. Un taxi est aussi **grand/grande/grandes** qu'une voiture.

DEMONSTRATIVE ADJECTIVES (THIS, THAT, THESE, THOSE)

Masculine	Feminine	Plural
ce/cet (before 'h' or vowel)	cette	ces

Ce/cet/cette/ces are translated into English as 'this/that/these/those' – e.g.:

ce livre – this/that book
cet hôtel – this/that hotel
cette chambre – this/that room
ces élèves – these/those pupils

INDEFINITE ADJECTIVES

autre – other – e.g. Les autres élèves étudient l'anglais. J'ai une autre copine !
chaque – each – e.g. chaque élève, chaque voiture
même – same – e.g. Il a vu le même match. Elle a la même jupe.
plusieurs – several – e.g. J'ai plusieurs jeux vidéo.
quelque(s) – some – e.g. Pendant quelque temps. Quelques élèves ont oublié les devoirs.
tel, telle, tells, telles – such – e.g. un tel garçon, de telles voitures
tout, toute, tous, toutes – all – e.g. tous les garçons, toutes les matières

POSSESSIVE ADJECTIVES

We use possessive adjectives to express ownership – e.g. my, your, his. Possessive adjectives must agree with the noun that follows them – *not* the person who 'owns' the noun – e.g. **mes parents** (my parents), **tes amis** (your friends), **notre professeur** (our teacher).

	Masculine	Feminine	Plural
my	mon	ma	mes
your	ton	ta	tes
his/her	son	sa	ses
our	notre	notre	nos
your	votre	votre	vos
their	leur	leur	leurs

GRAMMAR

Choose the correct possessive adjective to agree with each noun.

1. **Mon/Ma/Mes** tante habite en France.
2. **Ton/Ta/Tes** portable est super.
3. Je m'entends bien avec **ma/mon/mes** père.
4. **Ma/Mon/Mes** parents aiment aller au cinéma.
5. **Nos/Notre/Mon** amis sont très importants.
6. Combien de temps passes-tu sur **tes/ta/ton** ordinateur ?

ADVERBS

FORMING ADVERBS

Adverbs are usually used to add detail to a verb to express how, when, where or to what extent something occurs. In other words they describe how an action is done (quickly, regularly, badly, etc.) – e.g. Je joue rarement au tennis. (I rarely play tennis.)

Many French adverbs are formed by adding -ment to the feminine form of the adjective – e.g. heureuse → heureuse**ment**.

In French, adverbs are normally positioned after the verb (unlike in English) – e.g. Je vais **souvent** en ville. (I often go to town.)

COMPARATIVE AND SUPERLATIVE ADVERBS

As with adjectives, you can make comparisons with adverbs using plus que and moins que – e.g. J'arrive **moins rapidement** en train **qu'**en bus. (I arrive less quickly by train than by bus.) There is no feminine or masculine version.

Similarly, you can also use superlative adverbs – e.g. Aller au cinéma est l'activité que je fais la **plus régulièrement**. (Going to the cinema is the activity I do most often.)

ADVERBS OF TIME AND PLACE

Some useful adverbs include:

Place:

> dedans – inside
> dehors – outside
> ici – here
> là-bas – over there
> loin – far
> partout – everywhere

Time:

> après-demain – the day after tomorrow
> avant-hier – the day before yesterday
> aujourd'hui – today
> déjà – already
> demain – tomorrow
> hier – yesterday
> le lendemain – the following day

GRAMMAR

Choose the correct adverb from the list to complete each sentence.

1. Le concert se trouve _____ du centre.
2. Tous les concerts ont lieu _____.
3. _____ je suis allé(e) à une boum.
4. J'ai _____ assisté à beaucoup de concerts.
5. Pendant le festival il y a des touristes _____.
6. _____ nous irons au marché.

déjà   après-demain   loin   hier   partout   dehors

QUANTIFIERS AND INTENSIFIERS

Try to add detail to your French speaking and writing by including quantifiers and intensifiers – e.g.:

> assez – enough
> beaucoup – a lot
> un peu – a little
> très – very
> trop – too much

PRONOUNS

PERSONAL PRONOUNS

The words 'I, you, he, she, we, you, they' are pronouns. They are the subject of verbs.

Singular	Plural
je	nous
tu	vous
il/elle/on	ils/elles

On is a singular pronoun and is usually translated as 'we' or 'you' – e.g. On va au concert. (We are going to the concert.) Qu'est-ce qu'on peut faire ? (What can you do?)

Remember that there are different ways of saying 'you' in French. Use tu when you are talking to one person informally (e.g. a classmate, friend or family member) and vous when you are talking to more than one person. You also use vous (you) in formal situations (e.g. in a job interview, talking to your head teacher, talking to someone you don't know).

OBJECT PRONOUNS

There are two types of object pronoun: direct and indirect.

Direct object pronouns

These are used to replace a noun that is not the subject of the verb – using 'it' instead of the noun itself – e.g.:

- Je te **le** donne. I give **it** to you.
- Il m'**en** a parlé. He talked to me about **it**.

Indirect object pronouns

In French, sometimes we want to say 'to him/her/them'. In English, the word 'to' is often missed out:

> to him – lui
> to her – lui
> to them – leur

e.g.:

- I gave it **to him**. Je **lui** ai donné.
- She gives **them** money. Elle **leur** donne de l'argent.

The table below shows the normal order of pronouns. (1) and (2) are direct pronouns; (3), (4) and (5) are indirect pronouns.

1	2	3	4	5
me				
te	le			
se	la	lui		
nous	les	leu	y	en
vous				
se				

RELATIVE PRONOUNS

You use relative pronouns to link phrases together or to add more detail about the noun. They include:

> qui – who, which
> que – whom, that
> dont – of which, of whom

e.g.:

- Voici les enfants **qui** sont sages. Here are the children who are good.
- Voici les produits bio **que** vous cherchez. Here are the organic foods that you are looking for.

> ce qui – that which, what
> ce que – that which, what
> ce dont – that of which, of whom, what

e.g.:

- Dis-moi **ce qui** est arrivé. Tell me what has happened.
- Dis-moi **ce que** le médecin a dit. Tell me what the doctor said.
- Dis-moi **ce dont** tu as besoin. Tell me what you need.

The following relative pronouns are used with prepositions:

> lequel (m.) – (the) … which
> laquelle (f.) – (the) … which
> lesquels (m.pl.) – (the) … which
> lesquelles (f.pl.) – (the) … which

e.g.:

- Voici la table sur **laquelle** est ton portable. There is the table on which your phone is.

The above pronouns can also combine with à and de to mean 'of which' and 'from which':

> auquel (m.)
> à laquelle (f.)
> auxquels (m.pl.)

auxquelles (f.pl.)

duquel (m.)

de laquelle (f.)

desquels (m.pl.)

desquelles (f.pl.)

e.g.:

- Ce sont des choses **auxquelles** je ne pense pas. These are things that I don't think about.

Note: penser is followed by à so it becomes auxquelles.

POSSESSIVE PRONOUNS

Possessive pronouns are used when you wish to say 'mine, yours, his, hers', etc. – e.g.:

- Est-ce que c'est mon portable ? Is this my phone?
- Non, **le tien** est à la maison. No, yours is at home.

English	Masculine	Feminine	Masculine plural	Feminine plural
mine	le mien	la mienne	les miens	les miennes
yours	le tien	la tienne	les tiens	les tiennes
his/hers	le sien	la sienne	les siens	les siennes
ours	le nôtre	la nôtre	les nôtres	les nôtres
yours	le vôtre	la vôtre	les vôtres	les vôtres
theirs	le leur	la leur	les leurs	les leurs

DEMONSTRATIVE PRONOUNS

Demonstrative pronouns are used in place of a noun to avoid repeating the noun.

They are used in French to mean 'this one/that one/these/those' – e.g:

- Il prendra **celui-là**. He will have that one.

Masculine	Feminine	Singular/Plural	English
celui	celle	singular	this/that
ceux	celles	plural	these/those
celui-ci	celle-ci	singular	this one
celui-là	celle-là	plural	that one
ceux-ci	celles-ci	singular	these (here)
ceux-là	celles-là	plural	those (there)

INDEFINITE PRONOUNS

You might need to use the following indefinite pronouns when writing or speaking:

quelqu'un – someone – e.g. Quelqu'un a laissé le robinet ouvert.

quelque chose – something – e.g. J'ai mangé quelque chose de nouveau.

quelque part – somewhere – e.g. Quelque part dans le monde.

tout le monde – everyone – e.g. Tout le monde doit recycler.

personne ne – no one – e.g. Personne ne veut recycler.

EMPHATIC PRONOUNS

In French when you want to say, for example, 'at my house' or 'with her', and you want to use chez or avec, you need to use the emphatic pronoun – e.g. chez moi (at my house), avec elle (with her). See the table below for a list of emphatic pronouns.

moi	me
toi	you (singular)
lui	him
elle	her
nous	us
vous	you (polite singular/plural)
eux	them (masculine)
elles	them (feminine)

PREPOSITIONS

Prepositions are linking words which usually show direction, location or time. Unlike in English, in French there is often more than one way of translating a preposition. For example 'in' could be translated into French as en or à.

COMMON PREPOSITIONS

Before:

- avant (**+ time**) – e.g. **avant** le dîner (before dinner)
- déjà (already) – e.g. Je l'ai **déjà** vu. (I have already seen him/it.)
- devant (positional) – e.g. **devant** l'ordinateur (in front of the computer)

In:

- à – e.g. **à** Lyon (in Lyon), **à** la mode (in fashion)
- dans – e.g. **dans** un magasin (in a shop)
- en – e.g. **en** France (in France)

On:

- à – e.g. **à** gauche (on the left)
- en – e.g. **en** vacances (on holiday)
- sur – e.g. **sur** les réseaux sociaux (on social network sites)

VERBS FOLLOWED BY PREPOSITIONS

Verbs in French can often be followed by an infinitive – e.g. Je sais nager. (I can swim.) Tu veux venir ? (Do you want to come?)

Many verbs need a preposition when they are followed by an infinitive. Here are some of the common ones:

aider à – to help to
apprendre à – to learn to
commencer à – to begin to
continuer à – to continue
décider de – to decide to do something
inviter à – to invite to
réussir à – to succeed in
s'arrêter de – to stop (doing)
avoir l'intention de – to intend to
avoir peur de – to be afraid of (doing)
avoir besoin de – to need to

COMMON CONJUNCTIONS

Conjunctions or connectives are used to make extended sentences and to include more detail in written and spoken French – e.g.:

- Il a beaucoup joué au football **puisqu**'il voulait être footballeur professionnel. He played a lot of football since he wanted to be a professional footballer.

The most common are:

car – for (because)
comme – as
depuis (que) – since (time)
donc – so
lorsque, quand – when
parce que – because
puisque – since (reason)
pendant que – during, while
tandis que – while

TIME EXPRESSIONS

DEPUIS QUE – SINCE

Depuis is used with the present tense when you want to say 'has/have been' in a time clause – e.g.:

- Il a commencé à pleuvoir **depuis que** je suis sorti. It has begun to rain since I came out.

NEGATIVES

Remember the position of the negative in a French sentence! – e.g. Je **ne** joue **pas** sur la tablette. Here are some of the common negatives you will use.

French	English
ne... pas	not
ne... jamais	never
ne... plus	no longer
ne... que	only
ne... rien	nothing

Note: ne... que – e.g. Je **n'**ai mangé **que** des bananes. (I only ate bananas.)
Note: ne... jamais – e.g. Je **n'**ai **jamais** mangé de bananes. (I have never eaten bananas.)

VERBS

PRESENT TENSE

The present tense is used to talk about what usually happens – e.g. Normalement je joue au football. (I normally play football.), what things are like – e.g. Il y a mille élèves dans mon collège. (My school has a thousand pupils.), and what is happening now – e.g. Je fais mes devoirs. (I'm doing my homework.)

REGULAR VERBS

In French, many verbs in the present tense follow the 1, 2, 3 pattern below:

	Verb type	Example	English
1.	-er	donner	to give
2.	-ir	finir	to finish
3.	-re	vendre	to sell

Remember that each 1, 2, 3 pattern has different endings. Check out the following verb patterns.

1. donner – to give

je donne – I give
tu donnes – you give (singular)
il/elle donne – he/she gives
nous donnons – we give
vous donnez – you give (polite singular/plural)
ils/elles donnent – they give

2. finir – to finish

je finis – I finish
tu finis – you finish (singular)
il/elle finit – he/she finishes
nous finissons – we finish
vous finissez – you finish (polite singular/plural)
ils/elles finissent – they finish

3. vendre – to sell

je vends – I sell
tu vends – you sell (singular)
il/elle vend – he/she sells
nous vendons – we sell
vous vendez – you sell (polite singular/plural)
ils/elles vendent – they sell

IRREGULAR VERBS

Be careful! In French, there are many irregular present tense verbs which don't follow these usual patterns. The most common irregular verbs are:

aller – to go
avoir – to have
être – to be
faire – to do/make

aller – to go

je vais – I go
tu vas – you go (singular)
il/elle va – he/she goes
nous allons – we go
vous allez – you go (polite singular/plural)
ils/elles vont – they go

avoir – to have

j'ai – I have
tu as – you have (singular)
il/elle a – he/she has
nous avons – we have
vous avez – you have (polite singular/plural)
ils/elles ont – they have

être – to be

je suis – I am
tu es – you are (singular)
il/elle est – he/she is
nous sommes – we are
vous êtes – you are (polite singular/plural)
ils/elles sont – they are

faire – to do/make

je fais – I do/make
tu fais – you do/make (singular)
il/elle fait – he/she does/makes
nous faisons – we do/make
vous faites – you do/make (polite singular/plural)
ils/elles font – they do/make

GRAMMAR

Complete each sentence using the correct present tense form of the verb in brackets.

1. Je _____ (**chanter**) au concert avec mes amis.
2. Tu _____ (**finir**) tes devoirs.
3. Tu _____ (**choisir**) tes propres vêtements.
4. J'_____ (**avoir**) un bon style !
5. Je _____ (**aller**) à l'école en voiture.
6. Il y ____ (**avoir**) un restaurant.
7. Ma ville _____ (**être**) ennuyeuse.
8. Le musée _____ (**ouvrir**) à neuf heures.
9. On _____ (**acheter**) un billet au guichet.

REFLEXIVE VERBS

Present tense reflexive verbs follow this pattern:

> **se coucher – to go to bed**
> je **me** couche – I go to bed
> tu **te** couches – you go to bed (singular)
> il/elle **se** couche – he/she goes to bed
> nous **nous** couchons – we go to bed
> vous **vous** couchez – you go to bed (polite singular/plural)
> ils/elles **se** couchent – they go to bed

GRAMMAR

Put these phrases into the present tense in French.
1. vous (**se coucher**)
2. nous (**se lever**)
3. je (**s'habiller**)
4. ils (**se laver**)

PRESENT PARTICIPLE

The present participle is normally made by adding -ant to the stem of the present tense of nous.

Present of **nous**	Present participle	English
nous allons	all**ant**	going
nous regardons	regard**ant**	looking/watching
nous disons	dis**ant**	saying

There are also some irregular ones:

Present of **nous**	Present participle	English
nous avons	ayant	having
nous sommes	étant	being
nous savons	sachant	knowing

Present participles should be used in the following way using en – e.g.:

- Il est rentré du match **en** chantant. He went home from the match singing.

FUTURE TENSE

There are two ways of forming the future tense in French. You can either use:

1. The present tense of aller **+ infinitive** – e.g. Je **vais acheter** un nouveau portable.
2. Or add future endings to the infinitive* – e.g. **J'achèterai** un nouveau portable.

* Note than many common verbs (such as avoir, être, aller, venir, faire) use a different stem instead of the infinitive.

For -re verbs, the final 'e' is dropped before the endings are added – e.g.:

- Elle apprendra l'espagnol.
- Elle aura quinze ans.
- Il sera en retard.
- Tu iras au Canada.

The second form follows this pattern of endings: -ai, -as, -a, -ons, -ez, -ont.

GRAMMAR

Choose the correct word from the list to complete each sentence.

1. Je vais _____ un ordinateur.
2. Il va _____ sa famille.
3. Nous allons _____ dans un restaurant.
4. Elle va _____ un blog.
5. Je vais _____ un e-mail.

voir   lire   acheter   manger   envoyer

GRAMMAR

Match 1–4 to a–d.

1. J'achèterai
2. Je visiterai
3. Je sortirai
4. J'écrirai

a. mes amis.
b. avec mes amis.
c. un nouveau portable.
d. un blog.

CONDITIONAL TENSE

You use the conditional tense when you want to say 'would/could/should'. To form the conditional, use the stem of the future tense and the endings of the imperfect tense.

> je finirais – I would finish
> tu finirais – you would finish (singular)
> il/elle finirait – he/she would finish
> nous finirions – we would finish
> vous finiriez – you should finish (polite singular/plural)
> ils/elles finiraient – they would finish

GRAMMAR

Complete each sentence using the correct conditional form of the verb in brackets.

1. Nous _____ (**manger**) au restaurant.
2. J'_____ (**acheter**) une maison.
3. Il _____ (**habiter**) en ville.
4. Ils _____ (**visiter**) un musée.
5. Mes parents _____ (**vendre**) leur maison.

PERFECT TENSE

Perfect (past) tense with avoir

Most verbs are formed in the perfect tense using the present tense of avoir and the past participle.

> j'**ai** mangé – I ate
> tu **as** mangé – you ate (singular)
> il/elle **a** mangé – he/she ate
> nous **avons** mangé – we ate
> vous **avez** mangé – you ate (polite singular/plural)
> ils/elles **ont** mangé – they ate

Verb endings:
- -er verbs – e.g. manger → mang**é**
- -ir verbs – e.g. finir → fin**i**
- -re verbs – e.g. vendre → vend**u**

Perfect (past) tense with être

Be careful because not all verbs use avoir. The following list shows all the verbs that use the present tense of être to form the perfect tense. All reflexive verbs are formed in the same way.

> aller – to go
> arriver – to arrive
> descendre – to go down
> devenir – to become
> entrer – to enter
> monter – to go up
> mourir – to die
> naitre – to be born
> partir – to leave
> rentrer – to go back
> rester – to stay
> retourner – to return
> revenir – to come back
> sortir – to go out
> tomber – to fall
> venir – to come

As they are formed with the present tense of être, the past participles of the verbs will need to agree with the subject.

See the verb arriver below as an example:

je suis arrivé(e)
tu es arrivé(e)
il est arrivé
elle est arrivée
nous sommes arrivé(e)s
vous êtes arrivé(e)s
ils sont arrivés
elles sont arrivées

GRAMMAR

Translate the following into French using the perfect tense of the verb in brackets.

1. I did my homework. (**faire**)
2. I ate a sandwich in the canteen. (**manger**)
3. He studied in the library. (**étudier**)
4. The teachers gave a lot of homework. (**donner**)
5. We worked very hard. (**travailler**)

GRAMMAR

Complete each sentence using the past participle of the verb in brackets. Remember to make it agree.

1. Elle est _____ (**rentrer**) à la maison.
2. Nous sommes _____ (**arriver**) au collège à neuf heures.
3. Ils sont _____ (**entrer**) dans la salle de classe.
4. Comment es-tu _____ (**aller**) au collège ?
5. Je suis _____ (**retourner**) dans mon école primaire.
6. Ma sœur s'est _____ (**coucher**) tard parce qu'elle avait beaucoup de devoirs.

GRAMMAR

Complete each sentence with the correct form of être or avoir.

1. Elle _____ revenue dans notre classe.
2. Nous _____ pris l'autobus ce matin.
3. _____-vous entendu l'explication du professeur ?
4. Mes amis _____ arrivés pendant la récré.
5. Les profs _____ restés dans la salle des professeurs.
6. Il _____ décidé d'étudier les sciences.

IMPERFECT TENSE

The imperfect tense refers to the past – e.g. I was/I used to. The endings are: -ais, -ais, -ait, -ions, -iez, -aient.

Use the above endings with the stem of nous from the present tense:

Present **nous** form	Imperfect **je** form	English
nous donn**ons**	je donn**ais**	I was giving
nous finiss**ons**	je finiss**ais**	I was finishing
nous vend**ons**	je vend**ais**	I was selling

Note: this is the same for all verbs except être (for which the stem is ét- – e.g. j'étais).

GRAMMAR

Translate these sentences into French.

1. I was writing a blog every day.
2. I was going on holiday every year.
3. He was playing tennis every summer.
4. It was raining every day.

PLUPERFECT TENSE

The pluperfect tense is formed using the imperfect of the verb avoir or être with the past participle. Verbs use either avoir or être just as they do in the perfect tense – e.g. j'étais allé(e) (I had gone), il avait mangé (he had eaten).

TENSES WITH SI

Check the following rule of extended sentences with si:

• si + **present tense** (future) – e.g. S'il arrive, je te le dirai. (If he arrives, I will tell you.)
• si + **imperfect tense** (conditional) – e.g. Si nous venions, je te téléphonerais. (If we were to come, I would telephone you.)

IMPERATIVES (COMMANDS)

In French you can make commands by using the tu, nous and vous form of the present tense.

Remember to leave out the pronoun (i.e. tu, nous, vous).

Mange ! – Eat! (singular)
Mangeons ! – Let us eat!
Mangez ! – Eat! (plural)

Note: for verbs ending in -er you will need to leave out the 's' of the tu form – e.g. Tu vas → Va ! (Go!)

Translate these commands into French using the form in brackets.

1. Visit the museum! (**tu**)
2. Give me the mobile phone! (**vous**)
3. Let's take the road on the left! (**nous**)
4. Look right! (**tu**)
5. Turn left! (**vous**)

PASSIVE VOICE

The passive uses **être** with the past participle of a verb. It is used to say what has been done to someone or something. There are three forms:

- Present passive – e.g. **Le recyclage est fait.** (The recycling is done.)
- Imperfect passive – e.g. **J'étais respecté.** (I was respected.)
- Perfect passive – e.g. **J'ai été piqué par une abeille.** (I have been stung by a bee.)

PRESENT SUBJUNCTIVE

You will only need to recognise this tense at Higher level. It is formed by using the stem of the third person plural from the present tense:

Third person plural present	Subjunctive for first person singular
ils donnent	je donne
ils finissent	je finisse
ils vendent	je vende

The endings for the subjunctive are -e, -es, -e, -ions, -iez, -ent.

VENIR DE

In French, you can use **venir de** to say you have just done something. You simply use the present tense of **venir de** plus the infinitive of the following verb – e.g. **Je viens d'arriver.** (I have just arrived.) Or you can use the imperfect tense – e.g. **Je venais de partir.** (I had just left.)

PERFECT INFINITIVE

The perfect infinitive is formed by using the infinitive of **avoir** or the infinitive of **être** plus the past participle of the verb. It means 'to have done'.

It is most often used with the phrase **après avoir** or **après être** (after having done) – e.g. **Après avoir vu le film, nous sommes allés manger au restaurant.** (After having watched the film, we went to eat in the restaurant.)

Remember, when using **être** in the perfect tense, there will need to be agreement with the past participle depending on whether the noun is masculine, feminine or plural – e.g. **Après être descendues, les filles ont mangé le petit déjeuner.** (After coming down, the girls ate breakfast.)

VERB TABLES

REGULAR VERBS

Regular verbs (-er, -ir, -re)

Infinitive		Present	Perfect	Imperfect	Future	Conditional
parler – to speak	je	parle	ai parlé	parlais	parlerai	parlerais
	tu	parles	as parlé	parlais	parleras	parlerais
	il/elle/on	parle	a parlé	parlait	parlera	parlerait
	nous	parlons	avons parlé	parlions	parlerons	parlerions
	vous	parlez	avez parlé	parliez	parlerez	parleriez
	ils/elles	parlent	ont parlé	parlaient	parleront	parleraient
finir – to finish	je	finis	ai fini	finissais	finirai	finirais
	tu	finis	as fini	finissais	finiras	finirais
	il/elle/on	finit	a fini	finissait	finira	finirait
	nous	finissons	avons fini	finissions	finirons	finirions
	vous	finissez	avez fini	finissiez	finirez	finiriez
	ils/elles	finissent	ont fini	finissaient	finiront	finiraient
vendre – to sell	je	vends	ai vendu	vendais	vendrai	vendrais
	tu	vends	as vendu	vendais	vendras	vendrais
	il/elle/on	vend	a vendu	vendait	vendra	vendrait
	nous	vendons	avons vendu	vendions	vendrons	vendrions
	vous	vendez	avez vendu	vendiez	vendrez	vendriez
	ils/elles	vendent	ont vendu	vendaient	vendront	vendraient

COMMON IRREGULAR VERBS

Irregular -er verbs

manger – to eat
The verb manger only has one irregularity in the present tense **nous** form: nous mangeons.

commencer – to start
The verb commencer only has one irregularity in the present tense **nous** form: nous commençons.

appeler – to call

Present tense:

> j'appelle
> tu appelles
> il/elle appelle
> nous appelons
> vous appelez
> ils/elles appellent

Perfect	Imperfect	Future	Conditional
j'ai appelé	j'appelais	j'appellerai	j'appellerais

Irregular verbs with changes of accents

acheter – to buy

> j'achète
> tu achètes
> il/elle achète
> nous achetons
> vous achetez
> ils/elles achètent

Perfect	Imperfect	Future	Conditional
j'ai acheté	j'achetais	j'achèterai	j'achèterais

espérer – to hope

> j'espère
> tu espères
> Il/elle espère
> nous espérons
> vous espérez
> ils/elles espèrent

Perfect	Imperfect	Future	Conditional
j'ai espéré	j'espérais	j'espérerai	j'espérerais

répéter – to repeat

> je rép**è**te
> tu rép**è**tes
> il/elle rép**è**te
> nous répétons
> vous répétez
> ils/elles rép**è**tent

Perfect	Imperfect	Future	Conditional
j'ai répété	je répétais	je répéterai	je répéterais

Verbs with changing spelling

Some verbs which end in -oyer or -uyer change the 'y' to 'i' in the singular and the third person plural forms.

envoyer – to send

> j'envoie
> tu envoies
> il/elle envoie
> nous envoyons
> vous envoyez
> ils/elles envoient

Perfect	Imperfect	Future	Conditional
j'ai envoyé	j'envoyais	j'enverrai	j'enverrais

Irregular -ir verbs

courir – to run

> je cours
> tu cours
> il/elle court
> nous courons
> vous courez
> ils/elles courent

Perfect	Imperfect	Future	Conditional
j'ai couru	je courais	je courrai	je courrais

dormir – to sleep

> je dors
> tu dors
> il/elle dort
> nous dormons
> vous dormez
> ils dorment

Perfect	Imperfect	Future	Conditional
j'ai dormi	je dormais	je dormirai	je dormirais

ouvrir – to open

> j'ouvre
> tu ouvres
> il/elle ouvre
> nous ouvrons
> vous ouvrez
> ils/elles ouvrent

Perfect	Imperfect	Future	Conditional
j'ai ouvert	j'ouvrais	j'ouvrirai	j'ouvrirais

partir – to leave

> je pars
> tu pars
> il/elle part
> nous partons
> vous partez
> ils/elles partent

Perfect	Imperfect	Future	Conditional
je suis parti(e)	je partais	je partirai	je partirais

venir – to come

> je viens
> tu viens
> il/elle vient
> nous venons
> vous venez
> ils/elles viennent

Perfect	Imperfect	Future	Conditional
je suis venu	je venais	je viendrai	je viendrais

Irregular -re verbs

boire – to drink

> je bois
> tu bois
> il/elle boit
> nous buvons
> vous buvez
> ils/elles boivent

Perfect	Imperfect	Future	Conditional
j'ai bu	je buvais	je boirai	je boirais

croire – to believe

> je crois
> tu crois
> il/elle croit
> nous croyons
> vous croyez
> ils/elles croient

Perfect	Imperfect	Future	Conditional
j'ai cru	je croyais	je croirai	je croirais

dire – to say

> je dis
> tu dis
> il/elle dit
> nous disons
> vous dites
> ils/elles disent

Perfect	Imperfect	Future	Conditional
j'ai dit	je disais	je dirai	je dirais

écrire – to write

> j'écris
> tu écris
> il/elle écrit
> nous écrivons
> vous écrivez
> ils/elles écrivent

Perfect	Imperfect	Future	Conditional
j'ai écrit	j'écrivais	j'écrirai	j'écrirais

lire – to read

> je lis
> tu lis
> il/elle lit
> nous lisons
> vous lisez
> ils/elles lisent

Perfect	Imperfect	Future	Conditional
j'ai lu	je lisais	je lirai	je lirais

mettre – to put

>   je mets
>   tu mets
>   il/elle met
>   nous mettons
>   vous mettez
>   ils/elles mettent

Perfect	Imperfect	Future	Conditional
j'ai mis	je mettais	je mettrai	je mettrais

prendre – to take

>   je prends
>   tu prends
>   il/elle prend
>   nous prenons
>   vous prenez
>   ils/elles prennent

Perfect	Imperfect	Future	Conditional
j'ai pris	je prenais	je prendrai	je prendrais

vivre – to live

>   je vis
>   tu vis
>   il/elle vit
>   nous vivons
>   vous vivez
>   ils/elles vivent

Perfect	Imperfect	Future	Conditional
j'ai vécu	je vivais	je vivrai	je vivrais

Irregular -oir verbs

pouvoir – to be able to

je peux
tu peux
il/elle peut
nous pouvons
vous pouvez
ils/elles peuvent

Perfect	Imperfect	Future	Conditional
j'ai pu	je pouvais	je pourrai	je pourrais

voir – to see

je vois
tu vois
il/elle voit
nous voyons
vous voyez
ils/elles voient

Perfect	Imperfect	Future	Conditional
j'ai vu	je voyais	je verrai	je verrais

vouloir – to want

je veux
tu veux
il/elle veut
nous voulons
vous voulez
ils/elles veulent

Perfect	Imperfect	Future	Conditional
j'ai voulu	je voulais	je voudrai	je voudrais

IRREGULAR VERBS

Infinitive		Present	Perfect	Imperfect	Future	Conditional
aller **– to go**	je	vais	suis allé(e)	allais	irai	irais
	tu	vas	es allé(e)	allais	iras	irais
	il/elle/on	va	est allé(e)	allait	ira	irait
	nous	allons	sommes allé(e)s	allions	irons	irions
	vous	allez	êtes allé(e)(s)	alliez	irez	iriez
	ils/elles	vont	sont allé(e)s	allaient	iront	iraient
avoir **– to have**	j'	ai	ai eu	avais	aurai	aurais
	tu	as	as eu	avais	auras	aurais
	il/elle/on	a	a eu	avait	aura	aurait
	nous	avons	avons eu	avions	aurons	aurions
	vous	avez	avez eu	aviez	aurez	auriez
	ils/elles	ont	ont eu	avaient	auront	auraient
être **– to be**	je	suis	ai été	étais	serai	serais
	tu	es	as été	étais	seras	serais
	il/elle/on	est	a été	était	sera	serait
	nous	sommes	avons été	étions	serons	serions
	vous	êtes	avez été	étiez	serez	seriez
	ils/elles	sont	ont été	étaient	seront	seraient
faire **– to do/ make**	je	fais	ai fait	faisais	ferai	ferais
	tu	fais	as fait	faisais	feras	ferais
	il/elle/on	fait	a fait	faisait	fera	ferait
	nous	faisons	avons fait	faisions	ferons	ferions
	vous	faites	avez fait	faisiez	ferez	feriez
	ils/elles	font	ont fait	faisaient	feront	feraient

ANSWERS

SELF AND RELATIONSHIPS
Page 21
1. My aunt is funny, kind and sporty.
2. When I was younger, I had/used to have lots of friends.
3. My best friend gets on well with his parents.
4. What are the qualities of a good friend?

TECHNOLOGY AND SOCIAL MEDIA
Page 25
1. Contact friends, be independent.
2. Send SMS (texts), use social media, speak to friends.
3. b

HEALTH AND FITNESS
Page 31
1. Eating habits in France.
2. Eat lunch at 1pm.
3. Eat in front of the television.
4. Read or listen to music while eating.

ENTERTAINMENT AND LEISURE
Page 35
1. Jerôme
2. Lila
3. Lila
4. Émilie
5. Jerôme

Page 37
1. La semaine dernière, j'ai fait des courses en ville.
2. Le weekend prochain, j'irai au cinéma avec ma famille.
3. Quelle est ton émission de télé préférée ?
4. Je ne peux pas sortir demain, parce que j'ai trop de devoirs.

FOOD AND DRINK
Page 41
1. His grandmother.
2. Chocolate cake with strawberries.
3. Half.
4. In the family kitchen.

FESTIVALS AND CELEBRATIONS
Page 45
The music festival in Paris took place on the first weekend in June. I went there with my friends and we slept in a tent. It was the second time I had gone away without my family. It was such an unbelievable weekend! I would like to go back there next summer.

LOCAL AREAS OF INTEREST
Page 51
1. A
2. A
3. B
4. B
5. B

Page 53
J'aime habiter dans ma ville, parce qu'il y a b eaucoup de choses à faire pour les jeunes. Dans le passé il n'y avait pas de cinéma, mais maintenant il y a un grand centre commercial. À l'avenir, je voudrais habiter en France parce que j'adore la culture française.

TRAVEL AND TRANSPORT
Page 55
1. Information desk/office.
2. Opposite the restaurant.
3. Forbidden during the crossing.
4. Go outside.
5. Smoke.

LOCAL AND REGIONAL FEATURES AND CHARACTERISTICS OF FRANCE AND FRENCH-SPEAKING COUNTRIES
Page 61
Last year I went on holiday with my parents. We stayed with my aunt who lives at the seaside. We visited her in July. It was very hot. We really liked the

beach. The theme park was really great and I'd like to go back there next summer.

HOLIDAYS AND TOURISM

Page 65

1. Carl
2. Laetitia
3. Nathan
4. Mathieu

Page 67

1. L'année dernière, je suis **allé(e)** en Espagne.
2. Il **faisait** beau et le soleil **brillait**.
3. Nous **avons passé** deux nuits dans un hôtel au bord de la mer.
4. Normalement, je **fais** beaucoup d'activités nautiques.
5. L'été prochain, nous **voyagerons** en avion.

ENVIRONMENT

Page 71

to help
to protect
to reduce
to damage
to save
to pollute
to recycle
to destroy
to cause
to waste
to use

1. b
2. c
3. d
4. a
5. f
6. e

SOCIAL ISSUES

Page 75

1. Are you a pupil at a lycée? Are you aged between 16 and 18? Do you want to make changes?
2. 1,000.
3. Disadvantaged children.
4. Via the website.

SCHOOL/COLLEGE LIFE

Page 81

1. Next to Delphine, because the teacher tells them where to sit.
2. To avoid chatting.
3. No noise is tolerated/they are sent out.
4. Their surname and first name in capitals and their class.
5. Spanish.

SCHOOL/COLLEGE STUDIES

Page 85

1. a
2. b
3. c
4. c
5. b
6. c
7. c

EMPLOYMENT

Page 91

1. To work as an au pair/nanny. To improve her English/to earn some money.
2. She looks after her neighbours' pets. She enjoys walking dogs.
3. He looks after children and is a sailing instructor.

SKILLS AND PERSONAL QUALITIES

Page 95

1. c
2. i
3. h
4. j
5. a
6. d
7. g
8. e
9. b
10. f

POST-16 STUDY

Page 99

1. I don't know exactly what I will study next year.
2. In my opinion, sciences and languages are really important in life.

3. Chemistry and maths are subjects that go quite well together.
4. Unfortunately, I will have to work very hard.
5. If I have good marks, I will carry on with my business studies.

CAREER PLANS

Page 103
1. Germaine
2. Hervé
3. Régis
4. Annie
5. Paul
6. Hervé

Page 105
Aimerais-tu travailler à l'étranger ?

Oui, peut-être que je passerai un an en France comme secrétaire dans un bureau. Je ne veux pas être informaticien, mais j'aime travailler avec les ordinateurs. J'ai vraiment besoin d'améliorer mes compétences linguistiques. L'année dernière je suis allé en Espagne et je n'ai rien compris !

GRAMMAR

Page 113
1. Une voiture est plus **chère** qu'un vélo. A car is more expensive than a bike.
2. Les avions sont les plus **impressionnants**. Planes are the most amazing.
3. Un livre est moins **intéressant** qu'une tablette. A book is less interesting than a tablet.
4. Un taxi est aussi **grand** qu'une voiture. A taxi is as big as a car.

Page 114
1. **Ma** tante habite en France.
2. **Ton** portable est super.
3. Je m'entends bien avec **mon** père.
4. **Mes** parents aiment aller au cinéma.
5. **Nos** amis sont très importants.
6. Combien de temps passes-tu sur **ton** ordinateur ?

Page 116
1. Le concert se trouve **loin** du centre.
2. Tous les concerts ont lieu **dehors**.
3. **Hier** je suis allé(e) à une boum.
4. J'ai **déjà** assisté à beaucoup de concerts.

5. Pendant le festival il y a des touristes **partout**.
6. **Après-demain** nous irons au marché.

Page 126
1. Je **chante** au concert avec mes amis.
2. Tu **finis** tes devoirs.
3. Tu **choisis** tes propres vêtements.
4. J'**ai** un bon style !
5. Je **vais** à l'école en voiture.
6. Il y **a** un restaurant.
7. Ma ville **est** ennuyeuse.
8. Le musée **ouvre** à neuf heures.
9. On **achète** un billet au guichet.

Page 127
1. vous **vous couchez**
2. nous **nous levons**
3. je **m'habille**
4. ils **se lavent**

Page 128
1. Je vais **acheter** un ordinateur.
2. Il va **voir** sa famille.
3. Nous allons **manger** dans un restaurant.
4. Elle va **lire** un blog.
5. Je vais **envoyer** un e-mail.

1. c
2. a
3. b
4. d

Page 129
1. Nous **mangerions** au restaurant.
2. J'**achèterais** une maison.
3. Il **habiterait** en ville.
4. Ils **visiteraient** un musée.
5. Mes parents **vendraient** leur maison.

Page 130
1. J'ai **fait** mes devoirs.
2. J'ai **mangé** un sandwich à la cantine.
3. Il a **étudié** à la bibliothèque.
4. Les professeurs ont **donné** beaucoup de travail.
5. Nous avons **travaillé** très dur.

1. Elle est **rentrée** à la maison.
2. Nous sommes **arrivé(e)s** au collège à neuf heures.
3. Ils sont **entrés** dans la salle de classe.
4. Comment es-tu **allé(e)** au college ?

5. Je suis **retourné(e)** dans mon école primaire.
6. Ma sœur s'est **couchée** tard, parce qu'elle avait beaucoup de devoirs.

1. Elle est revenue dans notre classe.
2. Nous avons pris l'autobus ce matin.
3. Avez-vous entendu l'explication du professeur ?
4. Mes amis sont arrivés pendant la récré.
5. Les profs sont restés dans la salle des professeurs.
6. Il a décidé d'étudier les sciences.

Page 131
1. J'écrivais un blog tous les jours.
2. J'allais en vacances tous les ans.
3. Il jouait au tennis tous les étés.
4. Il pleuvait tous les jours.

Page 132
1. Visite le musée !
2. Donnez-moi le portable !
3. Prenons la rue à gauche !
4. Regarde à droite !
5. Tournez à gauche !